The Buy-To Manual

How to profit from buy-to-let property during the credit crunch and beyond.

James Collier

1

Income Disclaimer

This book contains business strategies, marketing methods and other business advice that, regardless of my own results and experience, may not produce the same results (or any results) for you. I, or my publishers, make absolutely no guarantee, expressed or implied, that by following the advice below you will make any money or improve current profits, as there are several factors and variables that come into play regarding any given business. There is a certain degree of risk associated with any business venture and this risk is yours alone. Any and all sums of money mentioned in this book should be considered as a guesstimate only and your earning potential should be taken on an individual bases, there are too many variables and factors for the values in this book to be considered as what you may be able to make/charge.

Primarily, results will depend on the nature of the product or business model, the conditions of the marketplace, the experience of the individual, the location of the individual, the local marketplace, and situations and elements that are beyond your control.

As with any business endeavour, you assume all risk related to investment and money based on your own discretion and at your own potential expense.

Liability Disclaimer

By reading this book, you assume all risks associated with using the advice given below, with a full understanding that you, solely, are responsible for anything that may occur as a result of putting this information into action in any way, and regardless of your interpretation of the advice.

You further agree that our company cannot be held responsible in any way for the success or failure of your activities as a result of the information presented in this book. It is your responsibility to conduct your own due diligence regarding the safe and successful execution of your design and decoration if you intend to apply any of our information in any way to your home and/or situation.

To the fullest extent permitted by law, the sellers are providing this written material, its subsidiary elements and its contents on an 'as is' basis and make no (and expressly disclaim all) representations or warranties of any kind with respect to this material or its contents including, without limitation, advice and recommendations, warranties or merchantability and fitness for a particular purpose. The information is given for entertainment purposes only. In addition, we do not represent or warrant that the information accessible via this material is accurate, complete or current. To the fullest extent permitted by law, neither the sellers or any of its affiliates, partners, directors, employees or other representatives will be liable for damages arising out of or in connection with the use of this material. This is a comprehensive limitation of liability that applies to all damages of any kind, including (without limitation) compensatory, direct, indirect or consequential damages, loss of data, income or profit, loss of or damage to property and claims of third parties. This VOLUME is sold for entertainment purposes only, and the author, publishers and/or distributors are not responsible for any actions taken as a result of reading this course.

Terms of Use

You are given a non-transferable, "personal use" license to this book. You cannot distribute it or share it with other individuals.

Also, there are no resale rights or private label rights granted when purchasing this book. In other words, it's for your own personal use only.

Table of Contents

1. Introduction

Publisher's note: The property market is constantly changing, fluctuating. Any property values, averages or such like contained in this book were believed to be correct at the time the author wrote it but they may have changed by the time you read it. Also any products offered by financial institutions that may be mentioned, property law that may be mentioned and anything else, was correct to the best of the author's knowledge at the time of writing but, again, may not be by the time you read this. You must always double check the facts and we recommend you seek professional advice before making any kind of investment. The author is not a legal or financial professional and nothing herein should be taken as professional advice.

Dear Fellow Investor,

Aspiring property tycoons usually fall into two brackets. Those that think becoming a successful buy-to-let (BLT) investor is easy money and there's nothing to it. Then there are those that think it's almost impossibly difficult to break into and make successful. The truth is, as you would expect, somewhere between those two extremes. Thankfully it's nowhere near as difficult as some people think but there are pitfalls and it does take some effort and skill.

This buy-to-let manual aims to expose some of those pitfalls so you can avoid them and teach you the skills you will need to make a success of your property empire!

The basic formula is very simple: purchase a property for a sum "below-market-value" (BMV) in an area where there is a healthy amount of demand for rental property at that time (we're not looking at areas that might one day have strong rental demand), let it out for an amount that covers mortgage and other costs and make sure that there is sufficient potential for both letting and capital growth for the next decade and beyond.

Another great thing about buy-to-let is that you can make substantial returns in both good economic times and bad. You may have heard of buy-to-let investors falling bankrupt left, right and centre and that property investment doesn't work any more and won't work again 'till we're out of recession and property prices start rising substantially again. Nothing could be further from the truth. Many property fortunes have been made in falling markets in the past and this time is no different. The people having to sell up and going bankrupt invested unwisely and didn't really know what they were doing. They were able to make money in a rising market but when things started to get difficult it all fell apart. This manual aims to teach you how to invest wisely, how to make money from property now, during a "bad" market and then how to make money in the next "good" market.

There are many reasons why a downturn in the market is a golden opportunity for investing in property. Some of them include banks selling off property they've had to repossess and developers desperately trying to sell off property they've built but can't shift because residential buyers may not be able to obtain a mortgage from a jittery bank or the deposit requirement is simply too much. These two alone present huge opportunities for buying property significantly BMV. Due diligence must still be used, though, to ensure that you can actually let a given property in a given area. No matter how big the discount you can get is, if there's no one who wants to rent that type of property in that area you will still come unstuck. You must *always* ensure as much as is possible that any property you plan to buy will be able to cover your monthly costs on it.

Buying to let is not any sort of get rich quick scheme. It is a long term investment of 10 years and more. As with any investment you must do your homework! You need to research a number of things that we'll cover in this manual to be as sure as you can be that a particular investment is going to stack up and is worth going for. If it doesn't, walk away, there are so many opportunities it doesn't matter. Never get "wedded" to the idea of a particular property, if the research says "no" then you must also say "no". Always remember that you're buying as an investment, not to live in your self.

The Basics Of "BMV"

No one wants to pay more than they have to whether they're an investor or a home buyer but buying Below Market Value (BMV) is very important to an investor. A home buyer may be willing to pay more for their dream property but an investor must not. It is critical for an investor to always remember that **the cheaper they buy a property the greater the return on the smaller amount of money they've had to put in becomes**. As well as the obvious benefits to paying less for a property there are also the advantages of lower exposure, reduced risk, and potential for quicker portfolio expansion.

Media outlets may be making a lot of noise about average price drops of fractions of a percent or even one or two percent but as investors we are looking for a far bigger chunk off the current market value. 10% is usually the minimum discount looked for. It might not sound very easy to find property at such a large discount. Who's going to sell a house that's already followed the market value down for a further 10+% off? Well actually lots of people for all sorts of reasons. These kinds of discounts are routinely found at auctions and from new-build developers keen to dispose of remaining stock.

What about funding you may be asking? We all know how difficult it has become in recent years to secure buy-to-let mortgages, especially for high loan-to-value ratios. Decisiveness and speed are important here so you can grab a mortgage deal when one does become available as their availability so often disappears again very quickly.

Don't Forget The 120% Rule

For me, it's all about whether the rental income will cover the mortgage when I'm analysing one of the 100's of weekly opportunities I see. But not just cover the mortgage, a little more than that as well, we're looking to make money here! If the numbers don't stack up I don't proceed with the deal As an example if I saw an opportunity where the mortgage would be £500 per month I would want to be sure that it would let for at least £600 per month.

Don't just fixate on the amount a property could rent for, you must also be as sure as you can be that it will actually rent. It might be "worth" a thousand a month but if no one wants to rent it then it's truly worth nothing. An empty property is costing you for every month it's empty so you need to ensure that there is strong demand for that type of property in that area to secure a tenant right away.

One of the best ways to find out which types of properties do best in which areas is to talk with local letting agents. They are in an unrivalled position to be able to tell you what current supply and demand is for different types of properties in different areas. This is one of the classic mistakes novice investors make. They simply look at the property and may be crunch some numbers but completely fail to investigate whether a property will let or not. There is absolutely no point in owning a property you can't let, it will simply cost you money and deteriorate as it sits empty.

Future Gazing

All indications are that property prices will remain flat for the foreseeable future or even fall in some areas, possibly to the extent of pulling the whole national average figure down. However, property prices will rise again and may be sooner than many of the doom-sayers think. It's just a matter of looking a bit more long term than the average tabloid hack.

Since you're learning how to be a savvy buy-to-let investor for the long term (and not one of those fly-by-night, rush in, make a mess of it, get out and throw their hands up saying this property thing doesn't work merchants!) you must do that homework we talked about earlier. Be as sure as any one can be that you're going to be investing in an area that is as likely as possible to enjoy steady demand for rental property and will likely see capital growth. We're talking medium to long term here, 10 to 15 years. Generally the plan is that rental income covers mortgage, management and maintenance costs etc. and the long-term capital growth goes into your pocket.

As well as talking with letting agents (remember, they will be happy to help you with this because they're hoping you will let your property out through them) and estate agents you should also pay your local council a visit to find out about future developments in the pipe-line. Not just housing though, new places of employment and retail. Also not just potentially positive development, also look to make sure you're not about to invest in an area that's going to have a new sewerage works, land fill site, airport, nuclear power station or other such development built right next to it. Get all the facts you can before taking the "go", "no-go" decision.

With Best Wishes,

James Collier.

2. Basics Of Buy-To-Let

For success in BTL it is essential to keep supply and demand at the fore-front of your mind. What is the demand for rented property in your chosen locality and how well is that demand being supplied at the present? The ideal answers to those questions are high demand and insufficient supply. Obviously we can't know what other buy-to-let investors are planning but as far as is possible think whether it's likely that situation is going to continue into the long term, not just the present situation.

Shine A Spotlight Onto Demand

It is vital that there is a strong demand for rental property in your chosen area or areas. It may seem obvious but many new investors forget that if there are no prospective tenants for a particular type of property out there then there's no market for it, prospective tenants are your market. Also, house buyer demand doesn't necessarily translate to rental demand for that particular type of property in that particular area.

As mentioned before, contact local letting agents, you can find them in online directories or in a paper phone directory such as Yellow Pages or Thompson Local. If you can talk to people who are members of a professional body like the Association of Residential Letting Agents (ARLA - www.arla.co.uk) so much the better. You want to determine from them who, what and where. *Who* is renting, your target market. *What* they're renting and *where* they're renting it.

For example, you may find a one bedroom flat that looks great on paper but when you find out about the area it may transpire that it's all families that live in that area, looking for family houses with a garden, close to schools and so on. A one bed flat would more likely be rented by a younger person who would prefer a more vibrant area close to pubs and cafés.

You may think I'm banging on about research a lot, and you'd be right. When you consider how much buying a property costs surely it's worth a bit of research to give your self the best possible chance of seeing a return on your investment?

You'd be surprised, then, how many wannabe investors do only perfunctory research or even none at all! These are the people who are now selling their portfolio and bolting the doors to keep the bailiffs out.

Many newbies immediately believe their local area is where to start, and it may well be, but without research first you won't know one way or the other. There are benefits to investing locally. You know the area so know where the better and worse parts of town are and it makes managing your portfolio easier as there's less travelling involved between properties but if your research shows rental demand is not strong in your area then it's not a good place to operate . You will need to look further afield.

When you start growing your portfolio of property you could be causing your self problems if rental demand is weak. Every property you buy in an area has an affect on your existing ones in that area, you could saturate demand pretty much by your self. Talk about shooting your self in the foot! This is why research is so critical. If the demand is strong enough then you can enjoy many years of expanding your property empire in an area. Also just because an area was a good proposition last time, do your research for every property you're interested in buying in case the area it's in has changed since you last researched.

Analyse Supply And Demand

The majority of first time investors make the mistake of picking a type of property to invest in, eg, family houses or student flats, and then investigate the supply of that type of property. It is staggering how many people attempt BTL in this way. Some of them are successful doing it this way but it's more by luck than judgement. Also during the buoyant property market just before the 2007 crash they almost had a "get out of jail free card" in their back pocket - prices were rising so fast that even if they couldn't let the property, as long as they hadn't spent too much on any renovations, they could sell it on to the next person wanting to try their luck in this way and at least get their money back or quite often realise a profit. In today's market this is obviously not going to work well.

In this market picking what you want without investigating the current market price for the type of property in a given area is unlikely to work out well and certainly not consistently. Demand is where to start looking, before supply. This is why a common new investor's approach of going to estate agents to see what's available (supply) is not a good idea. Go to letting agents and talk to them to find out what the demand is for, both type of property and location of that property. Remember, letting agents will want you to do well as they hope to build a long term relationship with you so they can continue to make money from you. Estate agents want to shift houses and aren't so interested in long term relationships.

Beware The Myths!

"My property has car parking and that makes it really attractive to tenants."

Possibly true, however it doesn't guarantee that your property will let. Let's take this example, if there is over supply of 3 bed detached houses and they're being offered to let for the same price you are attempting to attain for your two bed end of terrace you're simply not going to let it, parking or not.

These "extras" can lend you an advantage over other, similar, properties in the area if, and only if, there is demand for that type of property in the first place. No matter how "high spec" your property or what other extras it has you are unlikely to attract a tenant to live where they really don't want to. A really rough estate, for example. Another classic is the "nice view". A view, however 'nice', won't guarantee you letting your property out if there are too many similar properties or not enough demand.

Again, whilst easy access to public transport or near by arterial roads are advantages in high demand areas where supply is insufficient, it doesn't necessarily mean increased rent-ability across the board. You must focus on demand and supply first.

Be Watchful For Oversupply

Again this is about ongoing research. You don't want to end up buying a property somewhere where a whole load of other new investors have herded to. Often so called "up and coming areas" suffer from this phenomena of investor flooding.

A neat little trick for helping you understand rental supply and demand in a particular area is to monitor rental prices in that area. Generally, if prices are rising in an area it may indicate more demand than supply and vice versa. In the declining case you may discover that there's new development going on in that area. If this is the case, check out the type of development and if it's full of the types of property likely to be snapped up by investors it may be prudent to look to another area.

A twist on supply and demand in recent times has emerged where demand has been created by investors instead of prospective tenants seeking to let. This has led to the odd situation where builders have been building new property and selling it all to buy to let investors who then struggle to let the shiny new property they've just bought. Tenants will find that there are several pretty much identical flats available for rent in the same block or identical houses in a terrace or street. Then it comes down to price.

We return, at this point, to something I mentioned before, tenant demand comes right at the top of the check list before buying any property. No tenants wishing to rent that type of property in that area equals no rent. Simple as that.

Keep The Basics In Mind

As you've had drummed into you by now, buy to let is all about supply and demand. Different areas will have demand for different types of property so you need to match type and area. Some areas will have an over supply of certain types of property, under supply of others. Some will have over supply of everything, no one wants to live in that area, and if you're very lucky you'll find an area that has high demand and insufficient supply for all types of property.

Due to the nature of supply and demand the market in each area will be in a constant state of flux to a greater or lesser degree. Because of this, some investors will lose out whilst others will make a killing. You want to be in the "making a killing" group and as we've discussed the way to ensure this is as likely as possible is to do your research carefully before you buy and keep abreast of the rental market/s in your chosen investment area/s.

As buy to let investors we must follow the demand rather than telling people how they should live by buying a certain type of property and then trying to let it to them. To be successful in buy to let we need to look for rental demand first and then buy property to satisfy that demand. Not the other way round as so many wannabes do.

3. Borrow Your Tenant's Eyes!

You must look at prospective buy to let property through tenant's eyes. There are five key questions you need to ask yourself and answer satisfactorily before buying a property for your buy to let portfolio.

Question No. 1: Who Is The Tenant?

It is key not to make assumptions when answering this question. To be successful you need your properties to be rented out as close to 100% of the time as possible. Remember that when a property is empty it's not just the lost rental income you have to worry about. There are mortgage payments, utility bills, insurance payments, property security concerns and building condition deterioration as well. A common pit-fall for new buy to let investors investing in an area they know well is to assume they know who is renting in the area without actually checking to be certain.

For example many new investors in "University towns" automatically assume that they will be able to clean up with student lets. However, dig a little deeper and you may find, for example, that the majority of students at that specific University commute daily from home or, as is often the case with "campus Universities", there is sufficient University owned and administered accommodation available making the number of students renting from private land lords very small. You may find that there are other groups of people making up the bulk of the rental market instead. Immigrants just starting out or people on benefits just as two examples.

The best place to find this out? If you remember from above the answer is letting agents. I know I stated this before but it's worth reiterating. Make sure you speak with letting agents and not estate agents. Estate agents can tell you who's buying property but not who's renting it, they're not always the same types of people.

Question No. 2: What Type Of Property Does The Tenant Want?

Renting out property can be highly lucrative but only if you know who is renting what in your chosen area and then bringing that type of property to the market. Some newbies buy property that they like, that they'd like to live in, and dismiss property that they either don't like or at least don't love. This is a classic trap but one you are now aware of and can avoid. Buy rental property purely with your head, leave your heart at home when you go out viewing. Buying your own house with your heart is fine if that's in your nature but it has no place at all in investment.

To prove the above point, think about the kind of property you would like to live in. Now (depending on your age and circumstances) think about the type of property your parents or children would like to live in. I'll bet it's quite different to your ideal. This is a useful exercise as it helps you to see through other people's eyes. You need to buy the type of property that the type of person that makes up the demand in your chosen area wants and decorate/furnish it accordingly. You need to use that "mind's eye tenant" to help you make buying decisions rather than buying a property to suit you.

It's far easier to buy for your target tenant that you know exists in numbers than to buy a property you love and then attempt to find a tenant to rent it from you.

Question No. 3: Where Does The Tenant Want To Rent?

As the saying goes "location, location, location". This is just as important for prospective tenants as it is for buyers. This is largely common sense...

Where would a student want to rent? Within walking distance of the University or on a bus route to it more than likely. Obviously near or good transport links to the city centre with the pubs and clubs would be a benefit too.

Young professionals are going to want good transport links so they can get to and from work as quickly and easily as possible. Whether those transport links are public transport or arterial roads you must put this close to the top of the list when considering areas.

Family renters will want a mix of things, transport links are important for getting to/from work but being within the catchment area of a top-notch school will trump that. Walking distance from other amenities like parks, health centres and so on will also be very important for this group.

Answering questions 1 and 2 will give you a clear picture of the tenant and type of property and allow you to draw up a check list of what that type of person will be looking for in terms of location and you can hopefully also order the list by priority. This will help you select possibly locations. Question 2's answer will allow you to narrow areas down further as some of the areas that satisfy question 1 may not contain any (or at least not many) of the right type of property.

Some things for you to consider for your check list (you will be able to add more) shopping requirements, leisure facilities, night life, schools etc... Remember this is all done through your tenant's eyes, this is not a list of your requirements. You may like the idea of living within staggering distance of a pub but it's unlikely a family with young children would.

Question No. 4: What Comparable Properties Are Available In The Area?

This often overlooked question is actually very important. You need to speak with letting agents, look in the local paper, check on the Gumtree website and even pound the streets to find out what other properties like the one you're considering buying are available to tenants looking in that area. Many would be land lords only look at their property and ignore the fact that there are other landlords with other properties in the area. Often in the same block or street. It's back to that supply and demand thing again.

You've answered the previous questions so you know who's looking for what where. Now, how many other properties available to rent fit the target tenant in the target area? If there is insufficient supply to satisfy demand rents will be high and decent properties will not be empty long. Whilst I don't advocate the "slum landlord" approach to buy to let investing it is true that lesser quality properties can still be let in these areas of high demand and low supply.

Conversely in areas where either demand is largely being met or is low (but you remember from earlier we aren't going to be looking at low demand areas) rents will be pushed down and prospective tenants will get very picky very quickly. If they've a dozen properties to look at that meet their property type and location needs then it's the fine details that will make the difference. Quality of fit, finish, decoration and furnishing (in the case of furnished properties) can often have a big impact on the rentability of a property in these circumstances.

It's a double whammy, you'll have to spend more on the property to make it more attractive to tenants and spend more on advertising to get those viewings and all the time you'll only be able to achieve a lower rent.

Question No. 5: What Is Going To Happen In The Future?

Surely an impossible question to answer? It is but we still need to have a crack at it. Future gazing is notoriously difficult and unreliable but use common sense and have a go. We're talking 1 year, 5 years and 10 years plus.

Here's a simplified example to help you with your situation. A new University is founded so you know there's going to be an influx of students needing to be housed. Looking through the student's eyes the landlord knows they will want a property with low running costs and within walking distance of the University. Seems simple enough, buy a suitable property in the required area and let it to students. However, what the landlord needs to ask is whether that property has ongoing rental potential and capital growth potential.

What if the University decides to build more of it's own accommodation on campus? Does your property appeal to any other types of tenants (perhaps with a bit of work)? Hopefully the landlord considered this when buying the property in the first place and bought something that will appeal to more than students. Often "student areas" are towards the rougher end of town, did the landlord buy in an "up and coming area", perhaps an injection of redevelopment money is headed in that area's direction? This will help increase the property's value allowing the landlord to sell for a profit. A price rising area is important.

4. Diligent Due Diligence!

Many investors want to invest in property locations that are located a long way from where they actually live but are put off by that 300 mile drive! However, you may not need to actually go there to do your initial research. Now a days there's a huge amount of information available to you remotely.

Start To Find Out About The Town

Please note that web site designs change often so the below is correct at the time of writing but may be different at your time of reading.

www.maps.google.co.uk is a great place to start, it will show you where the town you're interested in is. It also shows you where it is in relation to other towns, what the transport links are like - motorways, railways etc. and you can also turn on the "satellite" view to see aerial photographs of the town. Use this with caution, though. If you see a load of burned out cars in your prospective areas that's naturally going to ring alarm bells but do keep in mind that the images are often many years out of date. Google only update the imagery very infrequently. Downloading the Google Earth application for your computer is another good way of doing this part of the research, often the imagery is different to that used on their maps website. Also the app has the image date visible (at the time of writing it seems much of the UK's imagery is of 2006 vintage).

information and leads to information. www.knowhere.co.uk may For major cities www.myvillage.com is a useful resource for both be an ugly site but it's great for getting information about a town. Often the comments can be quite "raw" to those easily offended but this also gives useful insight into the town and it's people.

For background research then www.thepaperboy.com/uk is an excellent place to start. Use the drop down menu under the heading "British Newspapers by City" to find local papers for the area you're planning on investing in. You will be able to read about planned local developments, roads, other infrastructure, new supermarkets, hospitals, schools and so on. Also you may be able to get a feel for which is "the bad end of town" to avoid although don't be swayed by just one story, bad things happen in "The good end of town" now and then as well, you need to build up a picture of the town and it's areas.

Gaining An Up To Date Picture Of The Local Property Market

Www.hometrack.co.uk used to have a free option which allowed you to get an idea of what's been happening in the local market in recent times. You entered a postcode for the area you were interested in and got a load of information. However, it seems to have become a paid only service. It's still worth mentioning as you may wish to make use of it, a relatively small amount spent now could save you losing a whole lot of money down the line.

Another avenue of research is local estate agents, the following websites will help you find them: www.naea.co.uk, www.teamprop.co.uk, www.relocation-agent-network.co.uk (formerly www.home-sale.co.uk) and the one that's been the most useful www.zoopla.co.uk/find-agents (formerly www.ukpropertyshop.co.uk and www.findaproperty.co.uk).

One other tactic you might like to employ is a good old Google (or whatever your favourite search engine is) search for the name of the town you're looking at and add "estate agents" to the end. But remember these are estate agents so the previous caveat applies. Some of the above sites allow you to switch to rental agent searches, using those will likely provide better results. Also you can modify your search to "name of town letting agents". Www.arla.co.uk is an excellent resource for finding letting agents in a particular area.

Property And Area Investigation

Having the postcode to hand for any property you wish to investigate makes life much easier. Don't be afraid to call up an agent or auctioneer to ask for the postcode if it isn't given in the property details. If, for some strange reason, they won't tell you you can use www.royalmail.com and their postcode finder.

Www.upmystreet.co.uk used to be the go to place for easy access to information on an area including crime figures, school performance, comments on what it's like to live in the area and so on. However, it now seems to have been bought out by Zoopla. Currently on the far right of the navigation there's a "Property Advice" menu, mouse over it to expand it and select the "AskMe Q&A" option. It's somewhat harder to navigate but you can still get some information here. The categories box is probably the best place to start, you can select crime and so on in there.

The information about and links to the local council don't appear to be available any more so you'll need to perform a web search to locate the website of the local council. Once there have a poke about press releases, planning applications and local plan information to try and feel out the local area. Pay special attention to the local plan and planning applications to try and find out if planned developments will have a positive or negative impact on your proposed investment. You may also find it a very useful investment of your time and a phone call to speak with the council about the most recent buy to let rules and regulations as they're constantly changing, the council will keep it's self abreast of these changes and also find out about any local by-laws that affect rental property.

Further Resources For Research

The government's own website www.direct.gov.uk is a wealth of information. You may be surprised to know that you can find information on local property prices on this government site, along with other things you'd more expect like local health service information, OFSTED reports for the local schools and so on.

Something important to note is that the house prices on the government site will be different to those found on the other sites previously mentioned and the numbers on those previous sites will likely be different to each other. This is because their source data is different so this gives you a range of prices for the area which can be quite a handy thing. However you need to be aware of this when tracking prices to see if they're stable, rising or falling. You must always compare prices at one time with prices at another time from the same site. There's no reason why you shouldn't track prices from several of the sites but always only compare the prices against others from the same site when looking for trends.

There's another source of house prices you might like t check out, the Land Registry – www.landregistry.go.uk – which is generally considered to be the most accurate and comprehensive data. For "today" price information, of course, local estate agents are the people to talk to.

Assuming that all your "remote research" has shown you that the area you're looking at is suitable for investment then the next stage is to physically go there and have a poke about the area your self. The government site can help you here again with it's journey planner or you can use one of the many other journey planners online, for example motoring organisations like the AA have them.

5. What's All The Fuss About "Off-Plan" And How To Do It?

What is "off-plan"? Off plan is where you agree with a developer or builder to buy a property before it's been built. You see the plans and agree to buy. Buying off plan allows you to buy at a considerable discount from the "retail" price that will be charged when the houses are built and ready to move into. These discounts have usually been in the 10 to 15% range in the past. Developers like to sell off plan even though they will realise a much smaller profit because of cash flow, mainly. They will have money in their hand to pay for building works. Also the other houses on the development will likely sell quicker when some of the houses occupied. Many people don't want to be the first or to feel like they're living in an empty building site.

The credit crunch has seen developers shedding staff, putting developments on hold and offering colossal discounts of 30% or even more on houses already completed. Discounts like this can offer phenomenal investment opportunities – but don't neglect to do your research as we've talked at length about before, if the demand isn't there then no discount is worth it – if you're able to move on them, getting a mortgage in these cases may prove difficult although things in this area are easing up a little now.

How Does Buying Off Plan Work?

A developer plans a new development, gets planning permission and so on and you, the investor, puts down a deposit on a unit (or more than one if you want to and have the means) after seeing the plans for the development as a whole and the individual units and an agreement signed for a discount (usually 10 to 15% as mentioned before) on the current market value of the finished unit/s. This built in equity (in a rising or static market, but don't forget that negative equity exists as well although the market would have to drop by the discount amount before the investor would be in a negative equity situation) makes buying off plan very attractive to investors.

Advantages And Disadvantages Of Buying Off-Plan

We've already talked about the discount but another financial advantage is that you'll usually only be required to pay a small deposit, something like 10%, and won't need to pay the balance until completion, usually several months down the line. Check whether the discount is non-refundable or not, so you know where you stand.

Recent market events not withstanding, residential property generally rises in value (certainly over the longer term) which builds in equity to off plan purchases due to the discount on market value and the market rise between agreeing the market value price and the market value when it's completed. A tidy profit can be had this way without any work at all even if you simply sell it when it's built rather than letting it. Also you may find these properties easier to let or sell as there is a section of the public who prefer a brand new property to live in than a "2nd hand" property. Assuming the build quality is decent then the maintenance costs of a new build should be non-existent for the first few years which is another plus.

As mentioned in the previous section it is possible to lose money buying off-plan even with the discount and so on if you buy either the wrong type of property or buy in the wrong area. This is why it's still vital to do your research and be prepared to walk away from what may look like "deal of the century" on paper. Another disadvantage of buying off-plan is the possibility of many investors doing the same thing in the same large development. This creates a situation where there's a sudden flood of (often very similar) rental property onto the rental market all at once or all within a short period of time.

Local pricing information is again critical when looking to buy off-plan because some developers will grossly over value their properties, offer you a big discount which actually brings the price down to it's genuine market value. If you know what similar properties are actually selling for in the local area then you're more likely to be able to spot an unscrupulous developer trying this one on.

The other obvious disadvantage to buying off-plan is that no one can 100% accurately predict what the local market is going to be like in 12 or 18 month's time when the property has actually been built. The local market could have dropped by then or the very development you've bought into could cause an over supply in the area which will push the market down it's self. So there are always risks in buying off-plan but there can also be substantial rewards. It's minimising the risks and spotting the genuine opportunities that separates the successful investors from the bankrupt ones! As you should know by now it's research that plays a large part in determining which type of investor you are.

Taking Advantage Of The Credit Crunch

With the "credit crunch" in full swing what is happening more and more often is many of these developers completing units with no buyers for them. Because of this some developers have been taking action to try and stay afloat during this crisis in the housing market. Action from which you can benefit. They are halting further work on their developments that are already under way and selling off the completed units with a deep discount, 20% and even more has been seen. Of course you still must do your due diligence, your research, to check demand and so on but these discounts can be great news for BTL investors. Don't get carried away though, I've said it before and I'll no doubt say it again later on in this book, no matter how deep the discount be prepared to walk away. If the demand isn't there or your research throws up another compelling reason not to buy, don't. If it is a genuinely good investment then bite their arm off and see if you can get an even deeper discount. If you have the finances in place and your research is very strong then this is probably the time to talk about bulk buying...

You may think that buying houses in bulk isn't possible or you don't have enough money to do it but what a lot of people don't realise is that when talking about something as expensive as a house "bulk" just means more than one. Don't be afraid to ask a developer if they can do you a bulk deal, a further discount. They will usually be very keen to be able to offload multiple units to a single buyer. Don't be shy about asking, remember two is bulk, you don't have to commit to buying half the development!

Some words of caution though, both your research and finances must be very strong. Never over stretch your finances, the market may go down further yet. The deep discounts will help to prevent a negative equity situation but it's still possible so make sure you can afford the repayments (and that you can get a mortgage in the first place). What some investors have been doing is to buy two or more with as large a discount as they can get then they sell one or more off immediately and keep some for letting. This way the built in equity of the discounts they have secured from the developer pays all their selling fees, legal fees for the lets and so on and some times even realise a few thousand profit in their pockets. Just something to think about. But always seek professional financial/legal advice before taking action.

Also you must treat anything the developer says with caution. Don't believe anything they say without verifying it with an independent third party. Developers tend to over value their properties so whilst a 20% discount may sound fantastic if the property is 20% over valued by the developer you're actually paying the real market value. May of the BTL investors that have bought off plan and not done well haven't checked the numbers and have paid over the odds for their property. Built in equity is very important in any market but especially in an uncertain one as we have just now. If the discount being offered by the developer turns out not to be a genuine discount - that the property was over valued by that much in the first place - then walk away.

It may sound like developers are a bunch of charlatans from what I've just said but (and there are some) this isn't necessarily the case. The usual reason for the above true market valuations is that in a rising market they "price ahead" to the value they think the property will be worth when it's completed. However, if the market levels out (or even goes down) between this valuation and the completion of the build then as an investor you could find your self with built in negative equity! At least in the short to medium term.

When buying these units for BTL purposes it's recommended that you go for a small site. This helps to keep a lid on supply, as long as you have strong demand these could make great investments. You don't want to be part of an investors (misguided) feeding frenzy and find you're trying to let a unit in a development that's been largely bought up by other investors and all of a sudden a couple of hundred units are dumped onto the rental market. You'll find achievable rents plummet and potential renters will be incredibly picky.

Tactics And Techniques

The first is to exchange early and complete late. The best deals can be negotiated with the developers the earlier you can get in (after you've done your research of course!) but a unit is harder to sell or let for the best price if it's in the middle of a building site. If the development has phased finishes you may be able to take advantage of this and buy a unit in a later (or the last) phase. The earlier you get in the biggest choice of plot you will have as well. Often you'll find that the "same" houses aren't actually the same because some will be on better plots than others.

Some plots will be bigger than others and often corner plots are more desirable as they tend to be bigger, more private and have less overlooked back gardens. Also don't forget to take the views into account. Take some time to really get to know the plans for the development, study them and make the best choice you can.

Developers will usually have artist's impressions of the finished units (but don't be fooled by the mother pushing a pram with a red balloon tied to the handle that they always seem to have) see if you can get the developer to agree to a walk round the site so you can really get a feel for how it will look, what the views will be like, how it fits in the landscape. As you're doing all of this keep your target tenant in mind, what would they think about all of these things, which plots would appeal to them the most?

Don't get caught in the "freebie trap". The old saying "you don't get something for nothing" is particularly true in the property market. Developers will often offer things like "deposit paid" or "cash-back mortgage" and whilst these sound great initially you will end up paying for them (possibly with interest, as it were) at a later stage. Usually the costs to the developer will simply be added onto the selling price. Calculate how much hard cash these offers are actually worth and then see how much of a discount you can negotiate off the price without having them. Take the best genuine deal. Keep in mind that a "cash-back mortgage" comes from the mortgage lender whereas a simple discount on the sale price comes from the developer so naturally the developer is going to be keen on pushing the cash-back mortgage.

This isn't to say that they're never good deals but it's important to know every one's true agenda before taking the plunge.

Something to check out in the early stages is whether the developer has a "funding partner" that will offer a mortgage facility to you. This can be an important sign for you as to whether both the developer and development are sound. Lenders will be quite happy to be associated with a good developer building a good development. If they have no funding partner you need to find out why not. There may be a legitimate reason for it but it's worth your while asking your self the "why not?" question and getting a satisfactory answer. Just because the developer has a funding partner that will give you a mortgage doesn't necessarily mean you should take it, though. Treat them as just another option when shopping around for the best deal.

Another thing that sounds like common sense but a surprising number of investors fail to do is keeping in touch with the developer between exchange and completion. They just assume everything is progressing to schedule and it's all fine. If you don't keep in touch you won't know 'till the completion date comes around, you're expecting to complete only to be told that there's been some problems and the roof isn't on yet. That can come as something of a shock!

If you notice any problems it's important to bring them to the developer's attention. They may already be aware but you won't know unless you tell them. It is very important to agree a "snagging day" with the developer before completion. A developer is much more likely to fix issues quickly and to your standards before completion than after. Afterwards many developers rapidly lose interest and want to get on with the next property. If they've left the site to start on the next project then heaven help you trying to get them to come back to fix a badly fitted door or whatever.

6. Below Market Value Repossessions And Where To Find Them.

We've already talked about buying BMV and repossessions can be a good way of doing this. If you're buying to let then the lower the price you can buy for means the bigger the yield will be for any given rental amount and if you're buying to sell then the lower you can buy for means the bigger the profit will be when you sell. With the credit crunch in full swing there are many properties being repossessed and this number is only rising at the moment which represents a tremendous opportunity for clued up investors. Often mortgage lenders will be happy merely recouping the outstanding balance of the mortgage rather than trying to sell the property for the best price. This can mean a property being sold for way below it's market value.

How does repossession work?

In most cases and in it's simplest form a repossession happens when the mortgage holder doesn't make their mortgage payments and they can't work out a resolution with the mortgage lender. Contrary to what some tabloid news papers might have you believe, repossession is not normally the first course of action and doesn't generally happen after just one missed mortgage payment. Usually the lender will attempt to work out a solution with the borrower but this is not always possible or there may not be a solution that will work in that particular circumstance.

Repossessions are not just a phenomena of the credit crunch or even just of a falling market. Repossessions happen in rising markets too. Often borrowers don't do their research properly and over stretch them selves or get a job in an area they simply can't afford to live in. Other common causes are the borrower being taken ill and unable to work, redundancy and divorce.

In law the lender must gain the best price they can for a repossessed property to maximise profits for shareholders, however, in reality a lender will usually be happy just to recover the outstanding balance of the mortgage and it's costs. If a decent chunk of the mortgage had been paid off by the borrower then this total will likely be less than the current market value of the property, some times substantially less and you can pick up a bargain.

Now is probably a good time to talk about moral issues surrounding repossession. Some people are squeamish about it, they feel it's "profiting from other people's misery" and on the face of it that might seem like a reasonable argument and make you feel uncomfortable. However, what people who say that are usually unaware of is the fact that the borrower is still liable for the full outstanding balance of their mortgage and costs until the lender has recovered the full balance and their costs. Usually this is until the property is sold. If the property can't achieve the amount of the mortgage (usually due to negative equity in a falling market, but not always) the borrower is still liable for the balance. But that's not so common.

Assume that the lender does cover the balance and costs when they sell the property, buy buying that property you are helping the borrower out of their situation and preventing them from a worse one. Yes it's a highly unpleasant situation for a borrower to find them selves in, regardless of the reasons for getting into that situation, and that situation won't be resolved until everything is paid off. They will be in a limbo until then. They may find it difficult to rent somewhere else to live until their property sells and their debt is cleared. Buy buying it you are at least freeing them up from that state, a state you did not put them in so there's no reason to feel bad about it. Something has caused them to be in arrears with their mortgage and their house is being repossessed, that's happening already and it's nothing you've done, you're not morally or actually responsible for that occurrence. Yes, you're planning on making a profit out of the situation but it's not a situation you caused.

If you still feel uneasy about buying repossessions then don't but you are discarding a potentially profitable vein of property to add to your BTL portfolio.

Another property myth that abounds is that there are secret sources of repossessions that the public never get to see. Some sort of secret list that only elite property gurus get to see. Complete rot! You just need to know in which public places these properties are sold. As I mentioned before, the lender has a legal responsibility to achieve the best price for repossessed property so there's no sense in secret lists with secret handshakes required to access them. They will sell these properties publicly such that they are seen to have tried to obtain the best possible price - whatever the market is willing to pay. This is usually via one of three ways, the traditional estate agent route, direct offer to the lender and of course an auction. We shall look at each in turn...

Estate Agents

Some local estate agents will sell repossessed property along side their "normal" property. These will not be marketed as repossessions, lenders don't want to advertise the fact they've had to repossess some one's home, it's bad PR for them. They want it done on the quiet, as it were. Also they would be likely to only receive ridiculously low offers if people knew they were repossessions and may not recoup what they need to which leaves the borrower still in the lurch.

There are signs that a property may be a repossession. Repossessions tend to be "Sold As Seen" although this is no guarantee that a house being advertised as such is a repossession but it can be a first clue. Also the boiler, toilet, sinks and so on may have "hazard tape", "condemned tape" or similar across them. They may be perfectly fine but it's often done to absolve the lender of any form of responsibility or warranty. Again this is not a hard and fast rule, they may be genuinely unsafe and condemned and it's a "normal" sale, not a repossession.

Some investors will walk or drive round the streets of a town looking for For Sale boards and then signs that the property is a repossession. These signs include no cars on the drive, no lights on at night or windows open, no comings and goings and generally no signs of life.

When they view the property it'll be the agent in attendance, the owners will not be. There is little or no furniture in the building. The property smells stale and there's post behind the door. All of these things are merely indications, though, there could be reasons for all of these things in a "normal" sale. The owner may have already moved house or may have moved in with a partner and they're selling off the extra house. They may have emigrated. There are many other perfectly normal reasons for this so don't assume it's a repossession just based on these signs.

Many investors will flat out ask the agent during a viewing "is this a repossessed property?". Some agents will tell you and others will say they can't answer that question, that usually (but again not always) means that it is. Many agents will tell you even though they know it will lead to a lower offer because they want their percentage cut of something now rather than a bit more at some indeterminate point in the future when they might get a better offer. If the agent won't tell you if it's a repossession and you happen to see a neighbour about after the agent has left then you can ask them if they know (probably best to open the conversation asking about what the area is to live in rather than diving right in with "do you know if it's a repossession?"), if they do (and neighbours often do) they will probably be only too happy to tell you and gossip about the previous owners. You can get a lot of information from a neighbour but you have to be careful, judge how the conversation is going. If they were very friendly with the previous owner they may be upset and angry about it as well so don't appear happy if it is a repossession.

Direct Offer

It may come as a surprise that occasionally repossessions are offered for sale in classified ads of local newspapers. Keep an eye on the local press and not just the property classifieds, repossessions can appear in other sections of the classifieds. Usually if they're not in the property section they'll be in the "legal notices" section, usually with the title "notice of offer". This is a formal legal notice that a lender has received an offer on a specific property. It is a repossession and the lender must be seen to be offering it to the public so they place these notices in a public place - the local press - to invite higher offers from the public.

There will be a closing date for offers, usually 14 days from the ad's publication. Sometimes the amount is published or can be found out by making enquiries but often it's done on a "sealed bid" bases where every one who wishes to bid bids the maximum amount they're willing to pay without knowing what any one else has bid and the lender will sell to the highest bidder. You will need to act fast on properties advertised in this way due to the closing date but do not short cut your research. If you've already done research on the area and this is a type of property you know has demand then you can proceed quickly, if not then you'll need to get your research done and make your decision before the closing date.

Some tremendous bargains can be had this way so it is definitely worth while keeping an eye out. Another good idea is to pursue the contact details of those who handle sales of repossessed properties, these are handy to keep in a notebook for future reference. Building rapport with these people can also be highly beneficial for the future.

Property Auction

We've looked at two other methods lenders use to dispose of properties they've repossessed but by far the most common method is via auction. Where these auctions take place varies greatly. Sometimes they're local to the properties being sold, usually only if there's a number in the same town, more usually they happen in the nearest big city and properties from that city plus all the surrounding towns and villages are sold in one larger auction. Sometimes London based lenders will just sell all their repossessions in a London auction regardless of where the properties are.

Phone your local and regional auction houses and try and get on their e/mailing lists for property auctions and have them post or email you catalogues for future sales. You can also do this for London auction houses that sell repossessed properties.

Not all the properties selling at auction will be repossessions. Look through the catalogues you receive and pay attention for phrases like "mortgagee in possession" and "by order of..." to identify repossessions.

There are a number of TV programmes that make buying property at auction look incredibly simple and massively profitable, and it can be. However, don't be fooled into thinking that every property that comes up for auction is going to be a bargain and you're going to make a killing on it either renting it out or selling it on. The basics of buying at auction are indeed simple. The auctioneer calls out the lot number and gives a brief description then the bidding starts. When the gavel comes down the person who bid the most has won the auction and is legally bound to pay for it.

However before bidding there are things you should do. You should attend a few auctions without signing up for a bidders number (you cannot bid without a bidders number so if you don't sign up for one there's no danger of you getting carried away and bidding) to get a feel for things. Get a copy of each auction house's terms and conditions. It's boring "legaleese" but you must read them thoroughly and understand them.

When you're ready to attend an auction to bid you will need to fill in a form to get a bidders number - you may be required to pay a deposit as well and there may be other hoops to jump through for a property auction, these should be detailed in the terms and conditions you've read so you'll know what they are - leave enough time to do all of this before the auction starts.

Before you leave your house for the auction you should decide on a hard maximum you will bid. Do not make this number up once already at the auction house. Write your maximum down and rigidly stick to it. Many a time people have contracted "auction fever", keep on making "just one more bid and I might get it" and end up paying way more than they wanted to, sometimes way more than they can afford and they end up in a very bad situation. You have been warned!

It is important to get the catalogue as early as possible which is why it's good to be on the auction house lists. You need time to evaluate each property, arrange viewings (sometimes they will schedule a viewing day for each property rather than allowing individual viewings), short-list properties, get surveys done, arrange finances and instruct a solicitor before you're ready to bid. Some auction houses will require proof of finances and other things before allowing you to sign up for a bidders number, take the relevant documents with you. Also you'll usually need a banker's draft for a deposit, make it 10% of your maximum bid amount. This is another good reason not to exceed your maximum bid amount in the heat of auction, your banker's draft won't cover the deposit required.

A final couple of points to note are that properties being sold outside of their area tend to achieve lower prices than they would if sold in their area. This means better bargains for you. For example if a property in Sheffield is being sold in a London auction. Properties towards the tail end of the catalogue can often go for less. There are two main reasons for this, firstly if there are a number of similar properties higher up the catalogue numbering people who are interested in that type may well already have bought and won't be bidding on another although if there are more bidders for this type of property than there are properties of that type then the last lot can spiral up as bidders who didn't bag one of the earlier ones are desperate to leave with a property. Remember your maximum when you see this phenomena happen. The other reason later properties can go for a bargain price is that buyers may have become bored and left (or cold and left, it's amazing how many auction houses are freezing cold) or may have spent their money and left or will bid a low amount but then run out of money and stop bidding.

7. How To Practice At Property Auctions

You may have come across the term "paper trading" in relation to financial markets but the same principles can apply to property auctions. For those that have not heard the term before, paper trading is where you pretend to trade, writing down buying and selling prices of whatever commodity on paper (a spread sheet can be used too) and you go through the whole process of evaluation etc. as if you were really buying but it's all on paper, you don't actually commit any of your real money. Another analogy would be a fantasy sports team.

For our purposes it's going to a few auctions with no intention to buy, just to get a feel for them and to see what you would have bought, and for how much, had you gone there to buy.

What Are Auctions Really Like?

Over the years a myth has taken hold that property at auction ends up going for prices above market value. The likely cause of this is people from outside of London attending London auctions crammed to the rafters with people and see the crazy London prices without having paper traded and without having done other research before hand. Imagine, as an example, some one from Sheffield going to a London auction without having researched London market values for those types of properties in those areas of London, they're going to get something of a shock when they see the London prices.

Another issue auction newbies often suffer is assuming that the auctioneer's guide price is the market value. Making that connection (falsely) can only lead to confusion and disappointment. Keep in your mind that they are not the same thing.

There are many reasons why properties are being sold at auction and often you won't know why ahead of time. If the property is up for auction due to a forced sale (eg. repossession) it will often achieve a low price but a unique property that's in high demand coming up for auction is likely to attract a lot of attention and the accompanying high bids. Often renovation projects come up at auction rather than going through estate agents (although many project properties do sell via estate agents) and can be quite unpredictable as to how much they sell for but the trend during the credit crunch has been for them to generally sell low.

Gather And Organise Your Information

It's a good idea to start a contacts list where you'll keep a record of auctioneers that might sell what you're looking for. Keep the company name, any names of people you have had contact with, their positions, phone extensions if you have them and email addresses. Also the company main phone number, address and email address. Have a section for notes too.

You'll want to gather details for local auction houses, regional auction houses - the nearest big city or cities to your target area, eg. Birmingham for Warwickshire and you'll also want to include London auction houses. Your local newspapers can be handy here as can local estate agents - ask them if they ever sell at auction and if so which auction houses do they use. It is not always the case but often the choicer properties will be auctioned locally, you'll likely find more forced sale properties up for grabs at the regional sales.

The London auctions will almost always be bigger in both terms of attendees and properties offered. It's important to monitor these auctions as well. Many first timers can be out-faced by a London sale, the scale of it and the relative glitz. They can also be misleading, as we talked about before, with London properties selling at London prices, however, properties from other areas might be more sensibly priced, you'll know when you see them, having done your research before hand.

It can be highly beneficial to build a good rapport with the auctioneers at the various auction houses and you should find out and note the closing dates for each sale - the last date when entries to the sale (properties being entered into the sale) will be accepted by them so you can get hold of the property particulars as soon as possible giving you as much time as possible to check them all out and decide if there's anything interesting to you in the sale.

Property Assessment

Once you know which properties are going to be in a sale you can start to assess them. Since you know your target market, area and type of property from your all important research you can quickly weed out those properties that are of no interest and have a much shorter list to check out.

For paper trading purposes pick 5 or 6 properties that interest you from looking at the photographs, catalogue description and assuming you can get them from the auctioneer the full property particulars. When doing this for real you may not have time to pick out so many but for paper trading try and go for 5 or 6 to gain a better picture of the market and it makes things more interesting any way. Also we'll be weeding some out as we go.

An important thing to note is that the photographs will likely have been taken to show the property in the best possible light. They're unlikely to show you the old caravan in next door's garden that's being used as a chicken coop, for example. Or the junky squat over the back fence! Note also that the catalogue description, due to space constraints, is merely a summary. This is where you need to ask for the particulars which contain more information. Sometimes the catalogue will include a floor plan and other times you'll need the particulars for that. Try and cultivate the ability to generate a 3D model in your head from these floor plans, it's really helpful if you can do that. Some people can do it naturally, most people need to work at it so don't be disheartened if you can't immediately do it.

It's amazing how many people contemplating spending tens or even hundreds of thousands of pounds at auction count a "drive by" as a viewing. If you happen to be passing a property you know is up for action by all means do a drive by viewing on it but only to see if it's an absolute no-no. It can be a quick way to discount a property but should never be used as a way to count a property in. You should always conduct a proper viewing.

The most common way for auctioneers to handle viewings is by way of block viewings or open houses. Eg. you book a spot on a block viewing or the house will be open and a representative there on a particular day or days, or a particular evening, morning or whatever. Occasionally they'll do individual viewings like an estate agent would but this is less common.

It's a good idea to see how the provided information compares with reality. This might allow you, over a number of viewings, to get a feel for which auctioneer's descriptions are closest to the reality and in which ways they tend to differ.

There's nothing to be shy about taking a tape measure with you (or a laser measure is even more convenient but more expensive) and checking the dimensions of the rooms. Note them down on the floor plan. Also take notes on the condition of each room, if you notice something in particular that would need repairing or replacing take a note of it and you can research costs when you get home. Another thing to note along with the negatives are any particular positives that jump out that might make it the better deal compared with an otherwise identical property. It's not uncommon for several properties that, on the face of it, look pretty well identical but there will usually be some features that make a property a better or worse value purchase.

Don't be shy about talking with the person who's in charge of the viewings. They're probably bored standing in an empty house for hour after hour and will welcome a bit of chat. Sometimes if you build good rapport with them they may let extra information slip that may be they shouldn't have. If it happens, note it but don't make a big deal of it, you don't want to put them back on guard, they may have more juicy info yet! That said, you should check it out to make sure it's fact and not just hearsay.

That Research Thing Again!

You must perform due diligence on each property ahead of the auction. If you know the market for that area well and the type of property well you already have much of the knowledge required. If it's been a while, though, since you did that research previously it wouldn't hurt to do it again to make sure you're up to date. You must work out the market value of each property you're interested in. As was said before, the guide price is not the same thing as true market value. A popular belief is that the reserve price, if a property has one (occasionally you'll find a property with no reserve on it), will be either the bottom guide price figure or a smidgeon above it.

Performing background research is hardly brain surgery but it is time consuming. You just need to talk with all the local (to the property, which is not necessarily local to you) estate agents to see what's available, view some properties and compare them. Ask the estate agent whether the asking price might be negotiable and see if they'll tell you what the seller's bottom line might be for each property. Remember they're interested in shifting houses rather than holding out for the best possible price, especially in a slow market.

This is about as far as you can go with paper trading without incurring significant expenses. If you were planning on taking things further with a view to buying, at this stage you would be asking the auctioneer for the legal pack which contains all of the paper work pertaining to the property. You would engage a surveyor to survey the property and value it, a solicitor to check the legal documents for general and special conditions of sale and other things. You would also need to arrange your finances, you remember from before, you'll need a 10% deposit to be handed over at the fall of the hammer and the rest of the money to be paid usually within 28 days but you'll know how long as you'll have already checked the particular auction houses terms and conditions, right?

Become An Attendee

You should make it your business to attend several auctions as a paper trader which is easier to do than attending as a bidder, you won't need to register, get a buyer's number (usually printed on a piece of card and laminated although more upmarket (or aspiring) auction houses will have the full-on wooden paddles you see on those antiques TV programmes), carefully check any last minute changes via the addendum or amendments sheet and of course your solicitor's phone number on speed dial in your mobile in case of last minute special conditions of sale being added or some other legal issue arising. But since we're just paper trading for now you can sit back and relax, a little.

You will have already done the preparatory work for the properties that interest you and you'll have a market value figure noted down next to each one. As those lots sell make a note of what it actually sold for. This allows you to compare when you get home and get a feel for where the best bargains are most likely to be had.

You want to arrive in plenty of time so you can pick up a copy of the addendum/amendments sheet to see what's changed and so you can get a decent seat or standing position. You may find the auction house isn't so busy but other times it can be hard to get into the sale room if you arrive late. Make sure you can see the auctioneer from your position.

Don't rely on lot numbers, make sure you know the addresses of the properties you're watching because it's not unknown for lots to be re-numbered at the last minute. A good auctioneer will often quickly mention there's been a change to the catalogue for the lot they're talking about but not always or they may have too many lots to get through in that sale to be able to spend the time so it is entirely up to you to stay on the ball and ensure you're watching the right lot. The most common amendment is probably the withdrawn lot. Usually the lot will just be shown as withdrawn in the amendments leaving other lots unaffected but occasionally an auction house may shuffle up all the other lot numbers although this is very rare.

Apart from getting a good viewing position it's important to arrive in plenty of time so you can watch the whole auction from start to end so you can learn as much as possible. You may be put off if the room is crowded and want to leave thinking that if there's that many people there's no point, all the lots will go sky high but don't be so hasty to give up, most of the attendees will not bid.

Yep, that's right, there will be other people just like you who are there just to watch, there will be others just looking for the "stupid cheap" bargains that very occasionally turn up but they don't have serious money to spend and will likely be out with the first bid. There are many more reasons for people being there but not bidding. Many times you'll also observe the crowd thinning out after certain lots have sold, those people came to the auction just for a particular lot and leave once it's sold.

Other interesting things to note are that most auction houses tend to list the more prestigious lots at the beginning of the catalogue and as you'd expect they tend to sell high. This obviously pushes the less prestigious lots (often out of town properties) to the rear end of the catalogue and they tend to sell lower.

Depending on the auction house you may also be able to negotiate a post auction deal for a lot that didn't sell during the auction it's self. Not all auction houses are open to this but it's worth asking to find out. May will entertain the idea as neither they nor the seller will particularly want to wait until the next suitable sale (which could be a month or two away) to try selling it again and the vendor may be willing to accept a lower offer just to get it sold. Once you've made your offer the auctioneer will usually need to go away and phone the vendor to see if they'll accept.

8. Auction Tips And Tricks For Bargain Bagging

It is possible to bag an amazing bargain at auction but it's also possible to end up paying way over the odds for a property at auction. This chapter should help you to avoid making that costly mistake.

Infrequent Auctions Frequently Lead To Bargains

You need to look for the one off and occasional auctions conducted by estate agents. That's not to say the regular property auctions can't yield bargains but these lesser known auctions can be a gold mine because they are lesser known, less competition. Around 80 or more auction houses in the UK stage regular property auctions - these are quarterly, bi-monthly and in some cases even monthly - and tend to attract a larger crowd, especially those in the larger cities. Some examples are Roy Pugh in Manchester, Bigwood in Birmingham and Allsop in London. These larger sales are usually very easy to find out about, a simple web search and a rifle through the phone directories should give you plenty to go on.

These sales tend to have more properties available (supply) but also tend to have more prospective bidders (demand). I'm using the terms supply and demand because it's just the same as when you're deciding on a property, you want low supply and high demand to keep rents higher. At auction it's the opposite, you want high supply and low demand to keep selling prices lower. A disadvantage of these larger sales is that because they're easier to find and have lots of property to sell there will likely be a lot of amateurs there, wannabe landlords. Not well prepared landlords like you will be by the time you get to an auction actually ready to buy. These amateurs often have the affect of pushing prices up. It is possible to find a bargain at these but don't go expecting one. You're generally better off frequenting the smaller occasional sales which are less likely to appear on the amateur's radar.

An example of these occasional sales would be Robert Ellis - an estate agents and chartered surveyor - held a sale in Nottinghamshire. Keep tabs on your target area, communicate regularly with the local estate agents and keep an eye on the local press for that area. When speaking with the estate agents, ask them if they keep a list of interested parties that they contact when they have one of their occasional auctions coming up, if they do get on that list!

Another couple of advantages to these sales are that often these sales aren't noticed by the professional property investors (surprisingly) and local buyers are often too "gun shy" to dip their toe into the world of property auctions.

Further Afield

The majority of investors buy either in their local area or in one particular area but buying out of your normal area can reap significant rewards. If you only concentrate on sales in one area then you could well be only seeing a fragment of the whole picture. Sales in your area may not be selling the absolute best properties for your area that are available. Again, as we've mentioned before, properties from a particular area often go to auction in London so if you don't keep an eye on the London auction houses then you won't even be seeing a considerable number of properties that are available in your area. This also applies to other auctions in the region, rather than just in your chosen town.

If you can buy properties at auction houses that are not in the location of the property for sale it's likely that it will sell for a lower price. For example if you are looking for property in Bolton, the prices for property in a Bolton auction house will likely be higher than that sold in Manchester. Don't limit yourself to the obvious, though, you may also find Bolton property for sale in Liverpool sale rooms and possibly even Birmingham sales. And of course there are always London sales. The further away a sale is from the location of the property the fewer potential bidders from the location are going to travel to it, although the fewer properties from that place are likely to be available. It's worth while keeping an eye on auctioneers in towns and cities in a 100 mile radius of your chosen investment location.

Shouldn't We Avoid The "Wrong Type" Of Auction?

The answer to that question is an emphatic no! The thing is, most auction houses will generally sell certain types property (the most common distinction being residential vs. commercial) and therefore gain a reputation for doing so. But auction houses are businesses and it's highly unlikely that a "commercial property auctioneer" is going to turn away the opportunity to sell a residential property. It's an opportunity for them to make a commission on another lot, they'd be crazy to turn that away. So if you're looking for residential property absolutely do not dismiss auctioneers that normally sell commercial property as being "the wrong type of auction" and of course the converse is true for those that wish to invest in commercial property.

A sale at Nelson Bakewell in London included between 5 and 10 residential properties in spite of the fact that they have a reputation for being a commercial property auction and as such they attract commercial lots from around the UK. A great many residential property investors missed these properties because they didn't include "commercial auctioneers" in their contacts data base. More fool them! With these residential properties and some commercial property with residential conversion potential a sale like this is a potential gold mine - the commercial investors weren't so interested in those lots and the residential buyers, largely, weren't even there.

So what makes the "wrong type" of auction? We've already talked about commercial vs. residential as that's the obvious one but let's get a little more subtle. "High class" auctioneers, it is often assumed, won't sell cheap "normal" property but that's simply not true, you can find mid-terrace 2 beds in the same sale as 15 bed country manors. We also return to the location issue, local auctions to one area won't necessarily only ever have property for sale in that area so do keep a look out for "local auctioneers" that aren't in your chosen area as they may occasionally have property for sale in your local area. Being seen as a "local auctioneer" means far fewer bidders from outside of that area are likely to attend.

Prepared For A Little Work?

The majority of property investors are hell-bent on buying a property that doesn't require any work that they can buy and immediately let out. This happens for many reasons including those that have so many properties they don't have time to do work on a property, amateurs that have decided they want to make a little extra money by buying a property and renting it out but they don't really know what they're doing so they think they're "playing it safe". Some have a limited budget and don't want to spend anything on repairs and upgrades and many other reasons.

It's usually a good idea to avoid these "move in condition" properties. If you go chasing these properties you're going to have wasted an awful lot of money on solicitors and surveyors doing things properly only to be out bid time and time again.

You will find there will usually be far fewer bids for properties that require some refurbishment. We're talking refurbishment here, not full scale renovation although these types of property can also offer large rewards but you really need to know what you're doing before taking on a project of that size. It's usually advisable to avoid these until you know what's involved and you're completely confident in doing it. A simple refurbishment should be within the grasp of most people. The cheapest way of tackling these is DIY - decorating and light repairs - but if that's not your thing and you don't know one end of a hammer from the other then you will need to factor in the cost of calling in tradesmen.

In general (but not always) you will tend t find these refurbishment projects at the smaller auctions rather than the "up market" city centre auctions although as we've discussed before it does happen.

Tap Into Late Additions

You may remember us talking about auctioneers putting the most attractive lots at the front of the catalogue to attract the best prices and as bidders leave throughout the sale prices tend to lower. Auctioneers often put the refurbishment projects after these and the renovation projects after them, a sort of "pecking order" if you like. Also the "wrong" lots will usually find their way to the back of the catalogue, eg. the "wrong type" of property, the "out of town" property and so on. This often helps you to bag a bargain.

A series of similar lots can also have a price reducing effect. An investor who owns a lot of similar properties liquidating their portfolio for some reason, a housing association selling off a group of it's properties and many other situations can cause these runs of similar properties to appear in auction catalogues from time to time. The interested parties will fight over the first few and as people buy they drop out of the running leaving the later ones to go for a lower price.

9. It's All About The Numbers

It is absolutely essential to sit down and crunch the numbers to see if you're actually going to make a profit and enjoy a positive cash flow. The last thing you want to do is blindly blunder into a loss making situation.

"Profit Budgets" And "Cash flow Forecasts"

There's next to no point in investing in a property if it isn't going to cover it's costs at a minimum and really you want to see a profit every month. If a property is only likely to break even on it's costs it could still be a good long term investment due to equity growth.

There are some that will buy a "loss making" rental property because the equity gain is so great and so fast that they will net a tidy profit selling it on in a few months or a year but no one really wants to subsidise their tenants for a prolonged period of time. This situation is very likely to occur in a generally falling or stagnant property market and it is definitely a more "advanced" strategy for those with deep pockets and plenty of bottle!

You should draw up a "profit budget" and a "cash-flow forecast" but don't worry if you don't know what's involved there, a quick search online should yield some sample documents you can download and use.

Profit Budget

A profit budget lays out what your estimated and actual income and expenditure will be over a period of time, eg. 6 to 12 months. It shows your overall profit/loss.

Cash Flow Forecast

Your cash flow forecast will show you when your estimated and actual income and expenditure occurs during the same time period as your profit budget and lets you know if you're currently in credit or debit.

Forecasting Your Income

We are putting aside the purchase price of the property for now as it's a "capital investment" and we're concentrating on the monthly financials. This is important because you need to be abreast of the monthly situation to ensure you're at least covering your monthly costs so you can profit from any equity gain down the line. If you have to sell prematurely due to monthly losses then you may end up making a loss on the sale too or at least not maximising the potential capital gains.

Firstly ask the question "is the rental income sufficient to cover (or better, exceed) monthly expenditure?" You also need to work out when the rental income is going to come in versus when your costs are going to go out and if any expenses have to go out (eg. mortgage payment) before the rent comes in you want to try and minimise the amount of time you're out of pocket. It is important to know both of these things so you don't find your self having a difficult conversation with your mortgage lender! A phrase you've seen me use before and will no doubt use again "it's surprising how many investors don't..." ...do these calculations first and end up in a world of financial hurt.

Remember speaking with all those letting agents during your research phase? Good. From them you will have a reasonable idea of how much rent you can expect from your property in the area it's in (if you did your research some time ago it doesn't hurt to call a few agents again and check to make sure the market hasn't changed in the mean time). Usually you'll want the rent to cover any mortgage payments, letting agent's fees (if you use one, more on this subject later) and other monthly costs and preferably leave some over each month to cover maintenance and so on.

It is also a good idea to factor into your budget some "dead time" when the property is empty. Often there will be at least a few weeks to a couple of months between tenants. I once lived in a flat that, according to neighbours, had been empty for 8 months before I moved in but then it was a fairly grotty flat in an unfashionable area of town. You shouldn't suffer such a long period of emptiness because... You've done your research properly! My landlord obviously hadn't.

If you can arrange things such that rent from your tenant comes into your bank before your mortgage payments go out it will make your cash flow much easier to manage, especially in the early days.

Forecasting Your Expenditure

You've probably had to spend some money to make your property suitable for letting - don't forget to check with the local council for the current rules and regulations regarding private lets (don't let them get confused with the regulations for private land lords letting their property to council tenants as they are often different) - so gather up all the receipts and group them under headings like "repairs", "decorating", "fixtures and fittings" and "furnishings" if you're letting it furnished.

There will be regular costs including maintenance, repairs,

renewals (hopefully less often), insurances and possible charges such as service charges and ground rents. Then there's tax on your profits. There will also be agents fees if you're using a letting agent that must also be taken into account.

Letting agents will usually charge an "introductory fee" and then monthly "management fees". The amount of the fee will depend on how much they're doing for you. These will usually be somewhere between 7.5% and 15% of the monthly rent charged to the tenant.

The tenant should be paying council tax, utility bills and TV license. With the exception of the TV license the agent will often contact the council tax office and utility companies to ensure the new tenant is being billed properly and you won't end up with demand letters for unpaid bills. Another thing the letting agent can do for you is to look at the list of expenses you've generated (add everything you can think of to it) and spot anything you've missed. If you're not using an agent then some one else can take a look at the list and see if they can see any omissions.

Assembling Your Profit And Loss Budget

As mentioned before you can search online and download a preprepared profit and loss budget and modify it to your needs. You will want all your income and expenditure headings down the left hand side of the sheet and name the next 12 months from your starting point along the top. Next the month headings are split into "estimated" and "actual". You have already forecast your income and outgoings so fill those columns in and you fill the actual columns each month as you track the situation.

As you can see this is more a forecast and comparison with reality over the time period (usually 12 months) concerned with overall finances than the exact timing of incomings and outgoings. That is the job of the cash flow forecast.

Assembling Your Cash Flow Forecast

This shouldn't pose any significant challenge as it's basically using the same information as the profit and loss budget you've just completed. The difference is that this one is concerned with the timings of the incoming and outgoing monies.

Since it's largely the same information as before you may be wondering why we're bothering with this but it is very important to know when money is coming in and going out. If a large outgoing is due out way before the rent is due in you could find a situation where you don't have enough money to cover the outgoing. That gets unpleasant quickly! At best you have to pay out of your own salary (if you have one) or savings (if you have any) and at worst you could, as I said above, find you can't pay. Using your credit card to cover this expense each month until the rent comes in is not recommended. This kind of issue might be manageable if you have the money to cover it but can you still cover it if your property is empty for a couple of months?

Don't forget the repairs and renewals that might be necessary between tenants as well. These are often forgotten about and sneak up on an unprepared landlord. Don't be that landlord.

You should be able to see how the investment is going to work out on a monthly basis by doing your cash flow forecast so there aren't too many nasty surprises (there are always going to be unforeseen circumstances crop up but you want to have as good an idea of how your cash flow is going to look every month as you can). Use the same headings as you did in the profit and loss budget but enter the details chronologically. You know when you expect to pay for things and when you expect to receive rent payments. Enter them all into the estimated columns. Fill in the actual columns as time goes on. If you actually receive a rent payment late then you enter it in the actual column when you receive it rather than when you expected to. This helps you to monitor your ongoing financial position.

10. Sitting Tenants

The term "sitting tenant" is used to describe that status of a property when it's sold. If you buy a property with a "sitting tenant" it means some one is already renting that property. You're buying the property and the tenancy from the current owner, kind of like buying a shop as a going concern. Sitting tenants have advantages and disadvantages. On the plus side the property is already let so there's no work to do finding a tenant and no empty period to financially cover but you need to proceed with caution, especially if the property is for sale at auction. The current owner may be selling at auction to put some distance between the seller and tenant and the buyer.

Scrutinise The Tenancy Agreement

It is vital to see the tenancy agreement between the current land lord and the tenant before you buy the property. It will show you what the landlord's and tenant's rights and responsibilities are and you can decide whether they're something you can live with or not. It might be a good idea to have your solicitor scrutinise it as well.

The age of the tenancy agreement is important, if it is post 15/1/89 then it will be an "assured" or "assured shorthold" tenancy which gives the landlord a greater ability to reposes the property once the period of the let has expired should the need or want arise. If a tenant has stayed ("held over") after the tenancy agreement has expired without it's renewal you will, as landlord, require a court order.

It is harder to reposes the property if a "protected" or "statutory" tenancy exists, either due to the provisions of the Rent Act 1977 or when such a tenant has "held over". Not only is it more difficult to evict these tenants the rent will be controlled.

These don't tend to be good investments but if you are tempted by a property and you discover one of these older agreements is in place you should definitely consult with your solicitor so that you fully understand all the legal implications and you can then make your buy/walk away decision fully informed by a legal professional.

When buying a property with a sitting tenant, regardless of which type of agreement is in place you must make sure that the vendor transfers the tenancy agreement over to you. Again it's a good idea to consult with your solicitor on how to do this and any pitfalls to look out for.

Check Out The Tenants

Make sure that the actual, real flesh and blood, tenants are who the lease says they are. It is not unknown (especially with student lets) for the tenants who's names are on the agreement to have moved on and there are other people now paying the rent. It's also a good idea to speak with the neighbours to check if they've had any trouble with the current tenants, this can be quite illuminating.

It may sound obvious but is sometimes a step overlooked - make sure that the current tenant is paying the rent on time every time. Get a reference from the seller and tell them that you need it to contain specific facts: 1) current rent owed, 2) date of last rent payment, 3) nature and amounts of any other charges, & 4) details of any unresolved disputes concerning the rent or the property.

If the seller is unwilling or reluctant to do this alarm bells should start gently ringing, if they come back to you with fuzzy generalities like "the tenant's a good bloke" the volume of those alarm bells should increase significantly. This is your business, you need hard business facts before you can commit a sum of money sufficient for buying a property. As with buying a non-tenanted property, don't be afraid to walk away from the deal if you're not completely comfortable with it. Also don't forget to consult with professionals as necessary.

Check Out The Property

Another obvious sounding step to take that a surprising number of people don't do... Check that the property is in good order. Go for a viewing just like you would before buying an untenanted property. Some wannabe investors just assume the property is good because there's a tenant in it. It could, in reality, be a vermin infested, rot riddled, damp sink-hole of a house. People are sometimes so desperate to rent something they'll settle for an appalling property or they may be trapped there unable to afford to move out for one reason or another.

Just as with other properties you'll need to have a structural survey conducted and in addition to this you will need to find out if the tenant has been keeping their end of the bargain when it comes to maintenance that they're obliged to carry out, or not. You can have your surveyor include in their report the general state of the interior decoration, fixtures and fittings and the garden if there is one along with all the structural stuff.

Going into any property deal blind or even partially sighted is never a good idea. Get all the information you need before going ahead.

Check Out Your Finances

There are financial implications of buying a property with sitting tenant that you may not be aware of. If you require a mortgage to buy the property the lender will demand information about the tenant and what they have/haven't been doing. How much information they require will vary from lender to lender so the more information you can gather during the previous two steps the better. Make sure you have this to hand when talking with potential lenders.

When you are drawing up your cash flow chart and profit & loss budget for this property keep in mind that tenants do move on and it's possible that the current tenant serves their "notice to quit" once you've taken ownership and you may be without tenant for a period of time which means no rent coming in to pay the mortgage and any repairs that are necessary. You'll need to fund advertising for a new tenant or engaging an agent to do it for you out of your own pocket. Ensure you have sufficient funds to cover these eventualities.

Return To Your Research

Just because there is a tenant now doesn't mean that you'll easily find another one to replace them were they to leave. You must still have done the same research as if it were an empty building before you decide to buy. Make sure it is easily lettable in-case the current tenant decides to move out. Or I should say for when the current tenant decides to move out as they surely will sooner or later. If you're very lucky later may be years and years off but with our highly mobile society today that's less likely than it used to be. You shouldn't buy a bad property in a bad area of town just because there is currently someone prepared to live there, you will almost certainly be a long time in finding some one to replace them.

You may also have different ideas for the sort of tenant you want compared with the tenant you've got. Your research may show that the property is better suited to a different type of tenant (may be after a little modification) that might pay more, for example the property may currently have a student in but with some upgrading and updating you could attract a young professional couple that will be willing to pay more for the property with a higher spec finish.

As always the information from your research including that from the current owner, tenant and neighbours is vital to your buying decision. Don't be scared to walk away if any of the information is telling you to do so. Conversely if the information you have all points towards going ahead then that can give you confidence in going ahead with the purchase.

11. Letting Agents

If you're going to use a letting agent then finding a good one is vitally important. There are many really great agents out there but there are also some that are, shall we say, less than good. Finding a good agent is not just about them getting you tenants and dealing with them for you but also keeping you informed about the constantly changing local and national rules and regulations that apply to BTL.

Estate Agents And Letting Agents, How They Differ

They both deal with property so surely they're the same thing right? Well actually no, they're quite different although some companies do both (usually two completely separate teams of people within the one company).

An estate agent is interested in selling properties for people. They have information on people buying and selling locally.

Letting agents are interested in finding tenants and managing rental property. They have information on people renting and letting property in the local area.

As touched upon earlier in the book the two groups of people - those wishing to buy and those wishing to rent - in any given area may not necessarily be the same. This is a mistake that many newbie BTL investors make, not making the distinction between the two, and they base their buying decisions on information from estate agents rather than letting agents.

Buying a property to let rather than to live in is very different. For example, a two bed mid-terrace with a long, well kept back garden. Some one looking to buy to live in might very well find this an attractive proposition whereas a prospective tenant may baulk at the thought of having to maintain all that garden. Also as landlord it's unlikely you will want to pay a company to maintain it either.

A further point to note when dealing with a company that's both estate and letting agent when it comes to buying BTL property. They are conflicted as they want to sell the property but may know that it'll be hard to let. This is, yet again, where your research comes in. Decide on the type and location of property and then go to estate agents to find them, go to a letting agent to let it for you when you've bought it.

How Do I Chose A Letting Agent?

Most people will talk to as many local letting agents as they can and then go with the one that gave them the best feeling and that is sometimes the only thing you can do but if you can talk with other BTL investors and get recommendations from then then that's so much the better. A word of mouth recommendation for an agent is invaluable.

When approaching letting agents during your research phase it's likely that they will have a pre-prepared landlord's pack available which details the rules and regulations for letting. It will also include, or the agent can tell you, the legal rights and responsibilities of both landlord and tenant. You will also want to ask them about who's renting what in the area, what these people are looking for that make one property more attractive than another to them and so on.

Having a checklist drawn up before engaging a letting agent is a good idea so you can make sure you ask everything you need answers for and observe everything you need to. There's nothing necessarily wrong with a new company but one with an established track record could be seen as "safer". Check out

their website, is it easy for a prospective tenant to use and is it
kept up to date? Do they have decent ads in the local press
regularly? Find out what other advertising they do. Get a feel
for their staff, are they friendly, courteous and knowledgeable?
Do they return calls promptly? Is their documentation clear,
concise and straightforward or is it complex, obtuse and
generally confusing? The same goes for their fee structure.

Are They Members?

Members of professional bodies such as ARLA - the
Association of Residential Letting Agents (www.arla.co.uk) -
that is, not secret societies! While your letting agent being a
member of such an organisation isn't a guarantee of trouble free
dealings it's true that the majority of problems occur when
"independent" and unregulated agents are used. These are also
more likely to be the ones that disappear over night. Don't take
an agency's word for it that they're members of one of these
bodies, go to that body's website and use their member search
facility if they have one or call them up to check if they don't.

You really want to chose an agent that has two years or more
letting experience although that is tough on the completely
legitimate new agencies. Ensure they adhere to ARLA (or
other comparable body's) guidelines especially those on deposit
holding, rent holding, separate bank accounts and so on.
Confirm that they have "professional indemnity insurance".

Assess Value Rather Than Cost

First decide what you want from an agent and then gather
quotes from the agencies that have migrated to the top of your
list via your discussions with them. Most agents are pretty
flexible in what they'll do for you, you can find the tenant and
have them manage the property, they can find you a tenant and

then you manage the property or they can do both for you.

When starting out it's usually advisable to engage an agent to both find you a tenant and then go on to manage the property for you. You may decide once you've gained experience to take over one or both of these duties or you may find you've become too busy with other things or with finding more property to add to your portfolio to want to deal with either so continue as you started with them doing both.

Now you know what you want from your agent, have told them what to quote for (and you must ask each agent quoting for the same thing or you can't compare their quotes properly) and have those quotes back, you can assess them. Don't just pick the one charging the lowest fees, that's cost, not necessarily value. This is a common mistake made by people, an issue not helped by a certain supermarket branding it's cheapest goods, regardless of quality, as "value".

Let's take the example of two quotes, X and Y. Y is a couple of percent higher than X (they will usually quote a flat fee and then a percentage of the monthly rent ongoing). X may not be offering everything you want and Y is so it's worth paying Y a little extra to get the services you need. Conversely Y may be charging more because they're offering services in their package that you don't want and X may be offering exactly what you want so there's no point in paying the extra.

Your Letting Agent Works For You, Use Them!

It's generally a good idea for a new BTL investor to use an agent for both finding tenants and managing the property, at least for the first year or two. You can learn a great deal from them and after some time has passed you can decide whether you have the time, ability and confidence to take on one or both of the tasks the agent is currently performing. Many landlords find that with smaller and locally concentrated portfolios they can take on one or both of the tasks but as portfolios get larger and/or more spread out this can become more difficult and many prefer to use an agent.

Something you may not have known, having an agent can make it considerably easier to procure a mortgage which has to be a big plus in favour of using an agent. It shows the lender that you are approaching your investment in a professional manor. They see using an agent who's a member of one of those professional bodies we talked about earlier much more professional than taking the DIY approach.

12. Were You Going To Make One Of These 5 Fatal BTL Property Investment Mistakes?

As you know BTL can be a fantastic investment for the short to medium term in rental income and long term in possible capital growth but as with anything there are risks and common mistakes people make. Hopefully I can help you to avoid these rookie mistakes...

Fixated On Capital Growth?

At some point in the future you may decide to "cash out" on a property. Sell it and take the profits from it's capital growth but in normal circumstances this is a long term prospect. If you bought well this will usually look after it's self over a 10+ year period.

In spite of the "credit crunch" that the media take such delight in doom-mongering over, residential property has always trended upwards. Yes it does go down in the short to medium term and it has gone down a long way in recent years, some say it will go down again in the next few, may be as much as another 35% but over the long term residential property tends to increase in price.

If you bought at the peak in 2007 you may be a long time

waiting to see any capital growth. If you bought after the price crash you may already have seen some capital growth but if not (and even with another significant drop, should it happen) it probably won't be too many years before you see positive equity returning to your investment. There are some that expect property prices to double in the next 10 years but of course that remains to be seen. Ask 10 industry experts and you'll get 10 different answers.

A few years ago government figures stated that 250,000 new homes are required every year in the UK to keep up with the nation's housing needs. In 2008 only around 80,000 were built. As you can see that's not enough and it's no wonder the average age of first time buyers is increasing. Recent figures said that the average age had risen to 34 for people moving out of their parent's house. With only a fraction of the required number of new houses being built this inevitably puts upward pressure on house prices. Even if we're not seeing too many effects of that right now over the long term that pressure is very likely to show it's self in actual prices regardless of any short term drop or "correction".

That's all long therm stuff, right now you need to focus on month on month rental income. You need to keep the rent coming in to cover the mortgage and other costs going out. So how on earth are you going to work out if your proposed BTL investment is going to pan out? In absolute terms you can't but the following simple formula should help you to be as sure as you can be.

Look at the price (or your maximum offer/bid amount) for a potential BTL property and multiply it by 0.85 to get 85%. That is probably the absolute maximum you'll be able to get as a BTL mortgage but the banks are currently running around like headless chickens changing the rules seemingly daily. That's why it is important to check with several lenders first to get an up to date idea of how much it is possible to get for a BTL mortgage.

From that figure work out the monthly repayment amount, let's work through an example...

Property price £125,000

85% = 106,250

Let's use an interest rate of 6.5% for a BTL mortgage (remember to check with lenders for a real, up to date, value): (6.5 x 106,250)/100 = £6906 per year which equals £575 per month.

Talk with letting agents in the property's area to find out what this property could realistically achieve in rental income. You will want to hear a figure of 120% or more of the mortgage payment amount.

So we need... (120/100) x 6906 = £8287 per year, which is £690 per month. That's the minimum number you need the monthly rental income to be. If the agent comes back with a number less than that you should be looking for a different property or revising your offer/bid amount downwards.

The lesson here is that you must focus on the rental income, not the capital growth side of things. Rental income is what will pay the mortgage and other bills in the short to medium term and the long term capital growth will generally take care of it's self.

Over Ambitious Rental Valuation?

It's not unknown for letting agents to give a somewhat "optimistic" rental valuation for a property. This is why you shouldn't just accept the first valuation as gospel. You need to get a number of rental valuations from different agents and also through your research gain a feel for what is a reasonable and fair rent for the type of property in that area. This may mean a bit of street pounding but a lot of the research may be possible to do online, on agent's websites and other places where lets are advertised like Gumtree.

Beware, though, that just because a certain rent is being asked for doesn't mean it's achievable. If you can find out what has actually let and for how much.

Doing this research is likely to give you a feel for which agents tend to pitch high on their rental evaluations to attract new landlords. It could be worth noting this in your growing database. Don't necessarily discount an agent that does this, just don't use their numbers! They may be, otherwise, very good and might be the agent you chose in the end, just be prepared to tell them to lower the rent amount to get a tenant in. However, it could be a sign that they're a bit sharp in their practice. You'll need to take a judgement on which it is.

You'll find, when selling, that estate agents do the same thing. Some will quote quite a bit higher than others to get your business. Pretty well every one will go with the agent that quotes a higher figure, it's human nature, but it's likely you'll actually get the lower figure any way (unless it's Scotland and you're listing "offers over" in which case, price too high and you just won't get any offers at all).

Offering a property to let is just the same, if you list it at the higher rent it could sit empty for some time which is costing you money each month and have to reduce the rent to the lower figure any way before you get a tenant. It would have been better to use the lower figure to start with and have a tenant in paying rent for those otherwise empty months. Usually the difference will only be a relatively small amount so having the property let for a little less per month works out more profitable than having it empty for months on end for a potential few quid a month extra when it is let. Assuming you don't have to go down to the lower figure to be able to let it. But it's quite likely you will have to do that any way.

Another problem with pitching too high and reducing later is that many potential tenants will be keeping an eye on property web sites and letting agent's windows over a period of time. They'll see the price reduction and assume you're in financial difficulties and quite desperate to get a tenant in so will press for further discounts. This has become especially true in these financially difficult times.

Does My Couch Look Big In this?

You should remember from previous chapters that when buying a property to let you are looking for different things as to when buying to live in. You may not like the property but it may be perfect for your target tenant. Well it's just the same when it comes to furnishing the property if you're letting it furnished. Your personal furnishing tastes are completely irrelevant.

Many landlords (especially newbies) will buy themselves new furniture and chuck the old stuff out of their house into the let property. This puts their interior tastes into the let property which may be totally wrong for the target market. Plus it will likely have at least some signs of wear and tear which for many target markets will be deeply off-putting.

Remember from a previous chapter when we talked about drawing up two lists to prove the point? One of what you want from a property and one of what your target tenant is looking for. Remember how different they were? The same applies for what decoration and furniture they'll like. Always remember that your taste is irrelevant when decorating and furnishing a property for let.

Generally speaking you will want to keep the décor and

furnishings clean, basic and cheap unless you're going for a high end target market but that market is relatively small so it's less likely you will be. You'll want to avoid heavily patterned carpets, wall papers and so on. Keep things neutral and plain. Magnolia is a standing joke but there's a reason it's the landlord's best friend. If you have to replace, for example, a 70's avocado bathroom suite with a plain white one it will give the room a much more stylish look and be more attractive to a modern tenant. After every tenancy you should assess the property and redecorate and replace as necessary.

Are You A DIY Manager?

It's tempting to save the money it would cost to engage a letting agent to find a tenant and manage the property and do it your self but this is usually a false economy. It's probably the biggest mistake newbie landlords make.

Downloaded generic tenancy agreements (that could be generations of law out of date) and home-brew tenancy agreements might very well not stand up to scrutiny in court should the situation arise. Of course you're going to be careful and nothing's going to go wrong... Until it does, horribly. This is where a properly written legally watertight agreement is essential and this is also where an agent will take care of things for you.

It's a common misconception of newbie landlords that letting to a friend or one of their friend's relatives is a great idea because "I know them, they're a decent sort". It's absolutely fine to let out your property to these types of tenants as long as you go through the process exactly the same as any other prospective tenant. The mistake often made is to not do the background checks, not get references and so on. This is when the temptation to use a generic agreement is the strongest even though it may not properly fit the situation or could be at odds with current law.

There are problems with managing the properties your self too. These problems are only magnified by distance. If your property is several counties over, for example, it's going to be something of a chore when that 8 a.m. on New Year's day call comes through about a broken down boiler.

Engaging an agent to find tenants for you, check them out and put together an agreement tailored to the exact situation that will be fully up to date with current law and will stand up in court is usually well worth the fee. Also bear in mind that letting agents have spent a lot of time vetting tenants so they become past masters at reading between the lines when it comes to references and answers to questions if they're interviewing tenants as well.

Having an agent manage your property for you means that it's them that will receive that New Year's day call and they will sort out a plumber to deal with it. You'll just have to pay the bills.

As we've discussed before not all agents are created equally and you should be looking for one that's ARLA or other professional body registered and vetted so you know that there's a code of conduct they should be abiding by, have all the necessary insurances in place and treat your deposit in accordance with best practices and a whole host of other things that protect you.

Do You Know The Rules?

Experienced BTL landlords often find it hard to keep abreast of the ever changing rules and regulations so as a newbie you're likely to struggle considerably in that respect, to start with. The key to this is ask. Ask your letting agent and the council local to your property and keep on asking them as the rules change over time. Ask your agent to keep you informed of any new developments that affect you or might affect you.

It's often seen by landlords as a chore but it is imperative that you do it because there are a lot of well informed tenants out there and things could go very badly for you if you haven't been keeping up to date with your legal obligations. Don't forget about compliance with fire regulations, for example, they're very different to those which apply to your own home. Some regulations can have implications far beyond financial ones. Breaches of some of the regulations carry custodial sentences. I'm not saying these things to put you off but so you know how important it is to keep up to date and implement what's necessary.

We've mentioned fire regulations already and related to that it's worth mentioning old furniture. You won't be using your old furniture because we've already talked about why that isn't a good idea but you may be tempted to save money by buying furniture at auction. It's not generally a very good idea to do this though because old furniture is unlikely to comply with modern fire regulations (these regulations also apply to things like curtains, a fact often overlooked). If you find modern furniture that is compliment and is in perfect condition then may be it could be a good way to save some money but you'd have to be 100% sure about it's compliance. It's far safer to buy new and I would recommend you do so, I do not recommend buying 2nd hand furniture.

Also related, in part, to fire are the regulations surrounding gas and electrical safety. Gas appliances must be routinely checked for safety including carbon monoxide emissions. You may find you legally have to install a carbon monoxide detector in each room where an appliance is present, check with your agent about this, also about smoke alarm provision - quantity, location and type. Safety checks also apply to electrical appliances.

These periodic checks all cost money which is why some landlords are tempted to skimp in these areas. If something goes wrong they will end up paying a much higher price. Plus, financial considerations aside, can you imagine living with the guilt of having electrocuted a tenant because you saved a few quid not having the appliances tested? Or blowing up half the street due to a faulty gas appliance? It's really not worth the financial saving.

Your agent should tell you about all the regulations your property, it's fixtures and fittings, must comply with . They may even be able to arrange for the required, qualified, tradesmen to come round, do the tests and checks and issue the relevant legal certificates. If they don't offer this service you will need to make these arrangements your self. Most tenancy agreements will require you to give a certain amount of notice to the tenant before the tradesman needs to access the property. When booking a tradesman visit on the phone make sure they understand it's a rental property and you need them to treat it as such and issue the relevant legal certificates for a rental property. As I said before, the rules governing private residences are quite different to those governing rental properties.

The regulations are changing all the time, usually getting tougher all the time, it is imperative that you keep on top of them.

13. A Taxing Matter

As the old saying goes, there are only two sure things in life, death and taxes. It's true. We all have to pay them but there's no point in paying more than you have to. We'll have a look at some of the ways in which you can minimise your tax bill.

Disclaimer Reminder

At the front of this book is a disclaimer section and in the introduction there are some notes but it can't hurt to re-iterate that the author and publishers are not any sort of professional, legal, financial or tax. They are not solicitors, financial advisers or tax advisers. You should always seek professional advice. Everything in this book is based on experience and research and should not be taken as "advice" in the legal sense. Engage professionals for that, they have the official qualifications and the insurances. Everything BTL related is changing all the time so you need to check information is up to date with relevant professionals. Also this book can only ever be general, your individual circumstances will be unique and require advice tailored to them. I'm reminding you of this at this stage because we're talking about the minefield that is tax!

Interesting

Most people buy a house and take out a mortgage where their monthly payments are both "principle an interest" which means they are paying the interest and they're paying off a little of the "principal", the actual money borrowed, so in 25 years time (or whatever the life of the mortgage) they will have paid off all that they have borrowed and all the interest owed on it. They will own their house outright. No more mortgage payments to make.

There is, however, another type of mortgage available. "Interest only" which is exactly what the name suggests. Your monthly payments are just the interest on the sum borrowed. The principal remains the same, it is not paid off a little every month.

The interest payments on a BTL mortgage can be off set against income tax. Payments against the principal cannot.

If you re-mortgaged your own home to provide the start up capital for your BTL venture (many people do this) you can also off set the interest payments of that mortgage against income tax.

Note that it's the purpose of the remortgage that's important. If you buy a property for cash and let it, then decide to mortgage against it to free up cash you cannot claim the interest payments against tax. This is why you need to sit down (with a tax professional and an accountant for preference) and really plan your financial strategy out before you start buying property. Take professional advice relevant to your individual circumstances as early in the process as you can. Don't be afraid to consult with them again further down the road as well.

What's In A Name?

"Repair", "Improve", what's the difference? Potentially quite a bit as far as your wallet is concerned. In a BTL property repairs are tax deductible whereas improvements are not. As an example, an electric heater packs in, fails safety checks or just generally is a bit tatty. You replace it with a comparable model, that's seen as a "repair" and should be tax deductible. You replace it with a model that has extra features or is more powerful, it could be seen as an "improvement" by HMRC and not tax deductible.

Depreciation Isn't All Bad

For those that aren't familiar with the term "depreciation", it is where the "value" of an item decreases with age. It may still be perfectly serviceable but it's value for tax purposes will have gone down. Even if it's been kept in a box and unused it will have depreciated as far as tax goes.

I'm sure you're aware of the depreciation cars suffer even if you weren't aware of the term. It's well known that as soon as you drive a brand new car off the dealer's fore-court it has magically "lost" a significant chunk of it's value (often as much as half) even though you didn't damage it in any way. It has depreciated and will continue to do so every year it gets older until it reaches scrap value pretty much regardless of it's condition. Obviously there are exceptions to this rule which are classic cars and some very exotic cars which appreciate (especially if they're a very limited edition) but for "normal" cars this holds true.

Furniture is one thing you can claim depreciation on in a BTL situation. As an example you might be able to claim 10% of the cost of furnishings in a furnished property against your tax liability. If you spent £1000 on them you would offset £100 (10%) against that year's tax bill. That leaves the "value" of those furnishings at £900 so year two's offset would be 10% of that, £90 and so it goes on.

Things get a little more complicated because your idea of furnished may not only differ from a tenant's idea of furnished but (for this section at least) more importantly it may differ from HMRC's definition of furnished. A sofa, bed, table and such like count as far as HMRC are concerned but fixtures generally don't. Make sure you know what's counted and what doesn't before you fit out your property to make it as tax efficient as possible.

Also, never try and pull one over on the tax man. You may get away with it but they have a nasty habit of finding out somehow and when they do it's a whole world of pain for you. Once found out it's unlikely you will ever get them off your back, you're likely to be audited every single year from then on and that carries costs as well as a lot of hassle, stress and heart ache. It's really, really not worth it. Yet another reason not to do it is that if you have a problem tenant things could "come out" during any legal proceedings or if they know what you've been up to they can rat on you. Even if they don't know anything they can say they do which has just the same affect. Don't give them the ammunition!

But that's an aside, back to depreciation. A rule of thumb I once heard (there could be exceptions as with any rule of thumb so check with your tax advisor) is "if it moves, claim for it". You can generally claim for something if it can be relatively easily taken out of one property and put into another. So obviously a fitted kitchen does not count or a bath tub, however a free standing heater would. Check the current rules for things like washing machines as they are transportable but they're also plumbed in.

"Allowable Expenses"

There are a number of expenses you will probably incur that are classed as "allowable expenses" such as (again, check as these change all the time) advertising fees, letting agency fees, legal fees for the letting agreement drafting and for any disputes with tenants that may arise, insurance premiums, accountancy fees for preparing your rental income accounts and the costs for any services you provide as landlord such as gas, electricity, water/sewerage and so on - this will depend on the tenancy agreement as to who's responsible for paying these.

Some allowable expenses are more obvious than others, some

that are often forgotten are rental insurance, service charges, ground rent and building insurance. VAT on any of these is also an "allowable expense".

This is why it is important to keep good records and keep those receipts! Don't throw them away, not even when the warranty on something has expired. That'll usually be a year but HMRC require that you keep documents for a number of years, the number is different for personal records than it is for business records. Check what the current time scales are, for business records it usually changes between 5 and 7 years (it seems to periodically change for some reason).

It's probably a good time to mention that even if you're using an accountant you must keep detailed records. If you just dump a shoebox of receipts and notes written on tatty bits of paper on your accountant's desk it's going to take them a lot of time to sort through it and make some kind of sense of it all. Accountants charge by the hour. The less extra work you make for them the less their bill to you will be.

I'd recommend you buy a box of plastic wallets or paper envelopes and label/write on the front the month and year and have one set per property. File receipts and notes relating to each property in the correct month's wallet/envelope. In cases where you've bought multiple items on one receipt for different properties take a photo copy (or scan and print) of the receipt sufficient for one per property and highlight the items on each receipt copy for the property who's file you're going to put it into. Also write a total (don't forget a share of the VAT and any P&P) for just those items. It's probably also a good idea to write a note on each one as to what you've done, that the items are for multiple properties and you've highlighted the relevant ones for that property. Do not think you're going to remember all these details when you might need them several years down the line.

Another reason to keep receipts and detailed records is that something you may not be able to claim for now might be claimable in the future. An example would be if you bought furniture at the beginning of your BTL investment. As we've discussed you can claim depreciation against income tax but you can't claim the initial purchase cost. However, it can probably be set against any Capital Gains Tax (CGT) liability that arises from selling the property in however many year's time.

CGT is something that a great many property investors don't think about, even highly seasoned ones, probably because it's usually only going to apply when you sell a property and want to pocket the equity (or capital) gains you've been building up over the years. HMRC want to pocket a chunk of them too.

The detailed notes you've been keeping along with your receipts are going to make your life a whole lot easier at this next stage. Use your notes to estimate totals for "repairs" and "improvements" separately. As per earlier you can claim the repair value against your rental income. Work out the percentage not claimed as repairs against expenses which can be a cost to deduct against CGT when the property is sold.

The best place to get current taxation information that you can be sure is accurate is HMRC's own website: hmrc.gov.uk . You can also visit one of their local offices, get their locations/phone numbers from either the website or local phone directory. They are usually very helpful.

Most people fear "the tax man" but in reality if you have a problem it is far better to go to them with it rather than waiting until they discover it and come knocking on your door. Usually you can work something out with them. Also don't forget that your tax advisor might be able to help you as well.

14. Yields

As you may have noticed the general media are pretty well completely focussed on capital growth and the lack of it in much of the country at present and on people finding them selves in negative equity. Ill prepared wannabe landlords selling up and making losses and so on. How investing in property is over, at least for the time being.

However, a slow down and even reversal in capital growth over the short to medium term isn't really a big deal for us, the well prepared BTL investor. The media are so fickle, when capital growth is around 10% they're shouting from the roof tops about the property market booming and if it falls to around 5% they're forecasting impending doom.

Yields are far more important to BTL investors. If you're not familiar with the term in relation to property investing, it's the return on the investment. How much the property is yielding per year. This figure is often somewhat different to any figure quoted in the media, on those rare occasions when they do actually mention yields. I'm convinced they're forgetting that as mortgages become harder to obtain and the average age of first time buyers goes up, as a result, this also means the rental market in an area usually becomes stronger which pushes up yields and they're using old data that doesn't show this.

In the long term, yes we are looking at capital growth as well but we have yields to look at before that and there's also gearing to throw into the mix which we'll discuss shortly.

Property Yields

The yield of a property is usually the "yard stick" used by investors to measure success and failure of their BTL properties. Let's look at an example. If you bought a property for £100,000 and let it for £8,000 per year that would make the yield 8%, not too bad. This is the calculation that the press will use to calculate yields when they do actually cover BTL. It's a very simple, yet effective, calculation to allow comparison of different properties, say you bought another £100k property but were only able to let it for £6k per year, that'd be a 6% yield, not quite as good as your first investment. There are other things to take into account when assessing an investment but yield is one of the most important.

This calculation is usually adequate for comparing potential investments to see which one you should invest your money in (or none of them and carry on looking for other options). It's from this calculation that the media come up with a rough average that allows them to declare whether property investment is the best thing since sliced bread or the devil incarnate that particular week.

Once investors gain a little experience they tend to quickly introduce "gearing" to their investment strategy. Gearing is basically using Other People's Money (OPM), for example a bank's money in the form of a mortgage, or some other investor. This allows a property to be purchased with significantly less money than you have. Andrew Carneigie founded his entire empire on OPM. In the case of a mortgage the money you put in is the deposit. Due to this relatively low amount of your own money invested it makes a big difference in the return you're making on your money and many property investors feel this is a better measure of investment success.

At the time of writing what mortgage lenders feel comfortable lending is changing practically every month. In the past they were happy to lend 85% of the value of the property, called loan to value (LTV) but after the 2007 shenanigans this figure has varied wildly. Whatever figure you find a lender willing to lend they will usually want to see a "rental coverage" of at least 120% (in the credit crunch some lenders have been increasing the rental coverage figure they want to see before approving a loan), this means that the monthly rent amount must be 120% of the monthly mortgage payment. To calculate this simply multiply the mortgage payment, eg £500 by 1.2, in this example that would give £600.

Gearing

Unlike the media whom, we've discussed, tend to only look at capital growth most of the time property investors like us look at both capital growth and the immediate rental income. The impact that gearing can have on both types of return is quite considerable as it can allow for larger portfolios.

Gearing is the name given to the strategy of using a small amount of your money to control a larger amount of some one else's money. It's not how much money you have that counts but how much money you can control. The simplest and most common method of gearing up your money is by using it as a deposit to control a larger sum of a lender's money by taking out a mortgage.

Another method is to find a cash rich, time poor person and have them invest their money into your property business, they will expect a return on it, just like the bank, so you need to be clear on how much that is before you work out whether a property is going to be financially viable or not before you buy it.

If we return to our previous example of yield without gearing, £8,000 annual rent divided by £100,000 purchase price, multiplied by 100 = an 8% yield. Now let's look at a geared example. Many investors like to gear their investment 85% meaning that they invest 15% of their money and use 85% of some one else's money. So £8,000 rental income divided by £15,000 money invested (15% of £100,000) multiplied by 100 = a 53% yield.

Obviously the mortgage must be paid, however, the capital growth hasn't been factored in either. The thing to remember is that whilst the yield calculation is a handy tool it's not the be-all and end-all that many self proclaimed experts say it is. Other things need to be taken into account to see the whole investment picture.

Long Term Strategy

Some people just want to have one or two investment properties making them a little extra each month and that's perfectly fine. I have no problems with those people, if you're one of them you're just as welcome here as the "serious" investors because you are a serious investor, serious about doing things properly too. Some "serious" investors are quite condescending of the "little bit extra" investors but it's just as valid as having a huge portfolio, each to their own and whatever suits an individual's circumstances best. We're all property investors together!

That said those investors may not find this section particularly relevant to their situation.

We'll look at an example over the longer term to show what gearing can do for you. Say you have £100,000 to spend. You could buy outright a property costing £100k, have no mortgage and, in keeping with the previous example, you manage an 8% yield. We'll use a figure of 5% per annum for capital growth. So, in 5 year's time (assuming it's continually let and rents remain the same) you will have taken in £40,000 in rent and the property will have experienced £27,628 increase in equity (compounded).

Now let's take that same amount of starting capital and gear it. With that amount you may be able to buy 6 properties (using 15% of 6 £100,000 properties plus a chunk for legal fees etc.) and using an interest rate of 5% makes the monthly payments £2125. If we use a rental cover figure of 1.3 that means rental income is £2762.50 giving a profit of £640 per month. Again using 5% for equity gains gives us £30,000 gain per annum (remember it's £600,000 worth of property to start with). In the same 5 years as the non-geared example you've taken in £38,400 in rents and equity gain of £165,768 across your 6 properties.

The total of £67,628 for the un-geared example is significantly less than the geared example's total of £195,768 over the same 5 year period. This illustrates the power of gearing.

15. Monitoring Changing Yields

We've just discussed what yields are and why they're an important number to know for each of your properties but the problem is, they're not a fixed value. You need to monitor each property's yield on an ongoing basis (this isn't as arduous a task as it may sound right now) so you know that all of your properties are still making you an amount you're satisfied with. If they're not it allows you to pick that up as early as possible and take action to remedy the situation.

If you've forgotten how to calculate yield see the chapter above. Many investors use 6% as their rule of thumb for investing or walking away. Obviously the higher the yield the better as far as rental returns go. The problem is that often investors will calculate this yield before buying and never again so they won't know what the current yield is. It's a mistake not to know what the current yield is for each of your properties.

Yield Changes

As time goes on the yield of a property will likely also change. If you bought that £100,000 property from a previous example and you bought really well - say the yield was a very healthy 10%, but is it really still 10%? If the property has doubled in value since then but the rental income remains the same the yield is now half as much, only 5%. You're not necessarily making the most of your money there. You could possibly use that £200k elsewhere to make a better return. If you don't keep tabs on your property's yield you won't know when your money could be working harder for you elsewhere.

Cashing in capital growth and reinvesting the money will sometimes make more financial sense than just sitting on a property taking the rent from it. Some people are happy to do that and pay the mortgage off from rental income over 25 or more years but if you're wanting to make as much as possible from BTL property investment you'll need to monitor your yields and take action as necessary.

If rental income doesn't keep pace with capital appreciation there will come a point when cashing in the appreciation makes more sense. A lot depends on the area and the type of property but the rental market will only tolerate a certain level of rent. If that rental ceiling doesn't keep pace with the capital appreciation you might want to look into banking that appreciation and moving onto another property or properties.

Broader Yield Picture

There are some price - supply - demand principles in the property market that pretty much hold true regardless of the market conditions. As purchase prices rise, yield percentages go down. As per the last section this is when a tipping point may be reached and a larger profit can be made from the capital appreciation rather than "straight BTL".

This has a knock on effect on demand for property. As yields decrease demand for property also decreases and prices fall. These falling prices then cause yields to increase which triggers an increase in demand for BTL property. You can see this is a cyclical thing.

Timing Embarkation And Disembarking From The Bandwagon

Investors who are yield driven will want to follow this merry-go-round cycle closely so they know when to invest, sell and then invest again. To do this you need to focus on supply, demand, price and what could be called "real time yield".

You will want to see a yield of 8% or more in a market that hasn't seen a strong and steady boom scenario yet before buying in. At the other end you need to sell before the yield falls below a point where the capital would do better elsewhere (a high interest bank account, for example). Perhaps something like 5 or 6% yield. When the yield has dropped to that kind of figure it's likely to go lower yet.

As we've mentioned before that's only one type of BTL investing - yield focussed - and they're not the only game in town. Real time yields can change relatively quickly and should be monitored regardless of your business model but are less important to people watching capital gains as well as yields. However, they must still be monitored and taken into account when planning to get in or out of a marketplace.

16. BTL Profits Over The Years

During the property market boom years pre 2007 property was often made out by the media and blokes down the pub to be a get rich quick formula (they were mostly focussing on renovating and selling on rather than BTL) but BTL is not a get rich quick scheme. It is a long term investment. In the short term rents should cover expenses such as borrowing and in the long term cash in the capital growth. This is why it is important to buy property that will be both easy to let and will appreciate sufficiently over time to make it worth while.

Immediate Cover

You can't just focus on capital growth, the rental income must cover your borrowings during the time (usually many years) you're waiting for that capital growth to happen and become large enough to make it worth while. It's important to have your BTL properties let out as much of the time as you possibly can for both financial reasons and for building fabric reasons. An empty building tends to deteriorate much quicker than an occupied one. Also, assuming you have a conscientious tenant, your tenant can alert you to issues with the property as they occur, before they turn into big (expensive) problems. With no tenants your investment has become a liability.

One way to help ensure that your property is let as much of the year as possible is to invest in property that appeals to a large and preferably growing market. As we've discussed before you need to look at the property through the potential tenant's eyes.

Revisiting a previous example, students. They will want to be within walking distance or on a bus route to their place of study and as close to the pubs and clubs as that allows. Even if you're quite familiar with an area it's a good idea to buy a street map of it so you can draw out an area to search for property in. If you are going after the student market don't forget to pick up bus timetables for all the routes that go through the area and then draw those routes onto the map as well. You could also print out maps from one of the various mapping websites. If you have the Google Earth app installed on your computer you can use it's "path" tool to find out exactly how far any given location is from any other via the roads or foot paths, not just an "as the crow flies" distance that drawing a circle on a map would give.

Five years is usually the absolute bare minimum amount of time you will need to hold a property to profit from BTL investment and more often the period is 10+ years. There can be rapid fluctuation in property values in an area but it's unlikely you'll see sufficient growth in a property's value to make the investment worth while in anything less than 5 years although it can happen. Because of this you need to look into the future as much as you can to "future proof" your investment as much as possible. Try and figure out how the market in that area might evolve over the next 10+ years.

Things like large employers expending or closing down will have an effect as will large new housing developments. Those are just two examples of factors that have the potential to drastically change the local rental market. Obviously it's not always that easy to guess whether an employer in the area is doing well or not but it may be possible to glean an idea from local gossip although gossip is just that and not to be taken as gospel. Housing developments are easier to forecast by looking at maps for obvious development sites, the local council's strategic plan and of course actual planning applications that will be available for viewing in the planning office. Talking regularly with planning officers may give you an additional heads up, also talk regularly with estate agents and letting agents.

A Tip For Finding Capital Growth

The student market is a very popular one with BTL landlords for many reasons, one of which is that capital growth of properties in university towns has tended to exceed the national average. In a five year period recently a 103% price rise has been seen across the country but prices in 10 of the 13 leading university towns have exceeded that.

A Halifax report a few years ago found that house prices in the towns with the top 20 universities in the UK showed price rises of between 82% and 87% over the preceding four years compared with a national average of 72%. There are other reports out there that all show the same picture.

Larger university towns are well worth looking at. They are usually large county towns, with good infrastructure, employment and entertainment provision. Do some research to check who is buying what and how fast each section of the market is growing. Many properties in large university towns are bought by parents of students and by post-graduates either studying for a masters or doctorate or who have found work locally and are staying. It is usually found that the most demand is at the lower end of the market, small flats and houses and larger houses either split up into flats or individual rooms being let, house shares.

Student Yields

As you're probably already thinking, there's always a constant stream of new students coming into a university town all needing somewhere to live. Most universities will have some accommodation available for their students to rent but they won't have enough for every one and not all students want to live in it any way. Some feel more independent renting their own place.

In recent years the government have been pushing to increase student numbers which has put upwards pressure on rents. Some university towns have seen rental increases of 10% and more year on year for several years.

That said it is still vitally important to do proper research - especially the supply and demand of property and for lets - before jumping into student lets with both feet because many of the major cities have seen a great deal of development and redevelopment in recent years which has, in many cases, caused a surplus of apartments and similar properties. This usually means it's quite hard to buy this type of property in these areas without exposing your self to somewhat higher risk. One solution might be to look at houses in and around university towns. Also don't discount ex-polytechnic towns. Don't forget to look for property along bus routes to these institutions.

Search online for an up to date list of the cheapest university towns to buy property in, a couple of years ago they were towns for the University of Lincolnshire and Humberside, University of Hull and the University of Bradford. Another avenue is to buy in towns where new universities are to be established although this is a little more speculative.

Scotland is another area that some investors are looking at and investing in due to the free tuition policy which is contributing to ever climbing student numbers. However a looming independence referendum is causing many investors from other parts of the UK to question the long term safety for them of investing in Scottish property.

17. How Can I Achieve Above-Average Capital Growth?

This chapter may initially strike you as being contradictory to what I've already said, about how important it is for a property to cover it's costs right now with the rental income and how some investors are too focussed on the capital growth. However, in this chapter we will be looking at capital growth because at some stage you're going to want to sell the property and realise a decent profit (many people sell their BTL properties when they retire, they are their pension pot). The watch word here is "balance". They're both important, the rental income and the capital growth. As far as capital growth goes, you want to have an eye on the long term capital growth potential of the area you buy into as well as the short term rental potential. It might be a hard idea to contemplate when you could be selling one, two or even three decades down the line but we have to try.

Features Of A Good Investment

This is a list of things that you'd generally want to see in a potential BTL investment property. Obviously it can't cover every circumstance but it's a good general starting point. The more of these attributes your location and property have the better.

The area:

- An "up and coming" area - these usually have good

transport links or have them planned/under construction. Quality amenities in the locality (or, again, planned).

- Has high quality academic institutions such as highly OFSTED rated schools, good universities and colleges.

- Historic towns and water-side locations are often popular.

The property:

- Under priced - forced sales usually produce the most under priced properties, often caused by people needing to move in a hurry for a new job some distance away or due to a separation/divorce and of course as we've spoken about before, repossessions.

- Well proportioned rooms - sufficiently sized to take a complete set of proper furniture.

- Potential for adding value - for example space to build an extension and/or conservatory or suitable roof space for a loft conversion.

- A decent sized garden. If really large perhaps it can be divided up to create another plot that can be sold or built on then let or sold.

- Off-road parking is more and more important these days especially in dense urban areas where it's at a premium. A garage is even better.

Finding A Great Place To Invest

Well established areas are sometimes a good place to buy for short term rental return. They do tend to be more expensive but often draw a certain type of tenant who's looking for the more fashionable bars, restaurants and shops. You will usually find cheaper property a mile or two away from these more fashionable areas. They may also have more potential for rent increases and capital growth because the demand for property in the fashionable area will tend to spread out as properties in the fashionable area become scarcer and more expensive.

As a general rule of thumb, an area with lower prices than a fashionable area in the immediate vicinity is probably going to be a good long term investment area as long as it isn't a case of the worst end of town is right next door to the best end of town or some other blatantly bad "feature". No matter how close to a fashionable area it is no one wants to live in "Scumsville".

Avoiding A Bad Area To Invest

It doesn't take a brain surgeon to realise that the list of "features" that make a bad, or at least mediocre, area to invest in is pretty much the opposite of the list for a good investment area. Here are some pointers for things to avoid:

- Over priced - you must compare apples with apples to see if a property or area is over priced or not. Check the prices of comparable properties.

- Overly fashionable buildings - something that's highly fashionable now will probably look very dated, unpopular and hard to sell by the time you come to move it on. Also people tend to be ultra conservative when it comes to property. Which, from an architectural point of view, is really boring. From an investment point of view unusual and non-traditional properties are usually best avoided.

- No private or off road parking. On road parking just outside the property is okay (people like to have a space they feel is "theirs" even if it isn't) but off road is better. Avoid properties with no near by parking.

- The bad end of town. Run-down estates with high unemployment are considerably more risky areas to invest in. Sometimes they can come good a decade or more down the line (check for planned regeneration projects) but these areas are usually in the "punt" category!

- Noisy neighbourhoods - whether it's major roads, airports, night clubs, pubs or something else people are increasingly valuing quality of life and like a quiet sanctuary they can return to after a hard day's work.

Some property specifics to avoid:

- Renovation projects - refurbishment (redecorating etc) is fine but a full blooded renovation can turn into a money pit.

- Over the shop. Residential units attached (not just over) to commercial premises don't tend to be so popular.

- Flood risk areas. Do a little research to make sure you're not buying on a flood plain or next to a river that is known to burst it's banks during very wet periods. Not only will this push your insurance way up if you can get insurance at all it means potential tenants could also do the same research and be put off. Then there's the problems of selling it on in years to come. Some mortgage lenders won't even touch a property in a flood risk area and this aversion is only increasing. If a potential buyer can't get a mortgage they will buy some one else's property that they can borrow against.

You need to be sure that a low priced area near a high priced one isn't low because it's in decline due to crime, social deprivation or such like. You're looking for a decent area that people will actually want to live in. Make sure you've done that all important research, don't just look at the prices and proximity to the fashionable area you're hoping to piggy-back off. As long as you make sure the area is decent and just under priced it will probably turn out to be a good long term investment as it's desirability increases due to the neighbouring fashionable area.

18. Trigger Events

A "trigger event" is something many investors look for when thinking about capital growth. It is a demand increasing something in an area. Often that something is an infrastructure project that will increase the popularity (and therefore value) of an area such as a tube line extension in London or an extension to the Manchester tram network.

If we take the London tube example, say a tube line is being extended to a densely built area where the space available for building more homes is little to none, the extra demand that the tube extension will create for property in that area can't readily be met which will often cause house prices and rents to rise.

Below are some of the more common trigger events to look out for. Don't forget that an area may be subject to more than one of these trigger events, that's great news, the more the better.

Transport Links

Often these are the biggest triggers for rent rises and capital growth. Whether it be a new road, railway or tram/tube it is transport that drives the economy and has a huge impact on property. The better the transport links to the major cities the more desirable the are becomes to commuters, this is especially so for London. Other trigger event developments are likely to follow new transport links which will usually snowball the effect on house prices/rents. New transport links can draw more property into "commuter land" that wasn't considered to be commuting distance from a major city before.

Development And Redevelopment Of Town Centres

Demand tends to be lower for property in a town with a horrible centre. Crumbling buildings and a generally dirty appearance are not appealing, neither is a high street full of charity shops, Pound shops and general tat-merchants. People want Waitrose, Tesco Express, Marks & Spencer, local boutiques and so on. Property prices often rise in the immediate vicinity after a centre has been redeveloped.

EU And Government Funded Developments

When the EU or Government funds some sort of development it will be a very definite project with publicly available information about it. You will be able to see exactly what is intended before work starts, this makes any investment that you might decide to make off the back of it less speculative as you know what's going to happen with the development. These developments also tend to be on a larger scale than the locally funded projects which in turn means they're likely to have a bigger impact.

Jobs

The arrival of a big new employer to an area is usually accompanied by a lot of local rejoicing. And you should rejoice too. All those new workers are going to need somewhere to live. Obviously it depends on the type of jobs being created as to how many will be filled by local people and how many will cause new people to move into the area but generally speaking a lot of new jobs means housing price rises. One thing to temper your enthusiasm, though, don't believe for one minute the number of new jobs the company tells the local press will be created. For starters, if they're building new premises for their operation they will include the temporary construction jobs in that number (if it's a long building project those builders will need to be housed if they're not local so that can be good for you letting property out) and they'll find other ways to inflate the numbers so it sounds better. There is no rule of thumb for guessing how many permanent jobs there will actually be as some companies are more creative in their hype than others. You could try halving the number for want of a better method.

Education

A new school can have an effect on property prices in an area especially where the existing schools are over subscribed or run-down and failing (check OFSTED). Find out what the catchment area for the new school will be and that will be the area you'll do your normal research on to see if it's a good investment area or not. Parents do move house to get into the catchment area of a good school. Of course, you won't know if a new school is going to be good or not so there is a fair chunk of speculation in this type of investment. That's why it's still important to do the normal research you would for any other idea.

Fashion

It may sound rather odd and definitely illogical (because it is) but sometimes an area will become "fashionable" for no readily identifiable reason. It's just the place to be for a certain section of the population, usually the more affluent younger buyers. These types of buyers also tend to be the ones that move the most. This is really quite speculative and takes a certain type of skill to regularly pull off. If you can identify an area in the earliest stages of becoming "fashionable" and buy in you can take advantage of often meteoric price rises. However, the area may not make it to full fashionable status and you could be left with an unsuitable property on your hands. Always, always do your normal research on an area regardless of any trigger event. These events do not guarantee success in any way, they can help though. Another thing to keep in mind with this type of trigger event is that just as areas that weren't fashionable can become so, fashionable areas can become unfashionable. You'll want to cash out of these areas before they become yesterday's news.

Identifying Triggers

Keep your eyes open. Monitor local news, TV, radio and press. Keep your ears open in the pub, talk to people when you're out and about and so on. A passing comment some one might make could be all the tip-off you need to get in early on in an area set to take off. However, when you hear about something don't ever take it as gospel. It could just be a rumour or someone misunderstood what they heard. Double check these things before you make any financial commitments. Even when you see something in the media, don't necessarily believe it. Check it out first. They could be misreporting the details or it may not be true in any form, it wouldn't be the first time the media have made stuff up or published wild speculation/rumour.

It doesn't hurt to jump in the car or onto the train and go to other towns in the area and see what's happening there. Pick up their local papers and talk to people, estate agents and so on. Listen to the gossip in the coffee shop etc. It may sound daft but "counting cranes" can sometimes give you a lead.

The national news can also help you identify trigger events. New government initiatives, funding and the like will all be publicised by our sound-bite politicians.

As we've discussed before, undervalued areas are often great hunting grounds for BTL investors and if you find one of these trigger events happening in an undervalued (in comparison to similar areas close by) area this can often lead to huge price rises. A little tip for you here, estate agents will often euphemistically refer to undervalued areas as "affordable" or even "surprisingly affordable". The trigger event combined with the affordability of the area will draw people in and create a local interest in the area which will in turn push prices up higher and faster than would otherwise have happened. As an example, Hoxton in London was undervalued a few years ago and became fashionable. Property prices rose 141% in 5 years. That was 37% more than the London average.

Ripples

The ripple effect is just like dropping a stone into a pool of water. Concentric rings ripple out from the point of impact. A property "hot spot" is the centre and the areas round it often benefit from it as well, the effects lessening the further away from the centre they are. A hot spot is expensive so people who want to be in that area but can't quite afford it will often look just outside that area, this increased demand will push those fringe areas up as well which in turn pushes those areas out of the price range of other people who want to be in the hot spot area so they, in turn, will look a little further out again and so it goes on.

Prices in hot spots tend to level off once they have surged in price and as a rule of thumb, the quicker the surge the quicker the levelling off will happen. This happens because people are priced out of the hot spot quicker and look elsewhere, they ripple out. Look at towns and villages within about a 10 mile radius and you'll observe the effect. An example of this a few years ago would be Leeds. Prices increased quickly and this rippled out to Harrogate and other places in the vicinity. Obviously the better the transport links are between an area and a hot spot the bigger the ripple effect is going to be on that area.

19. Trigger Event Due Diligence

Spotting a trigger event can be quite exciting and the urge to move on this newly acquired information is strong but you must do your due diligence first. Whilst a trigger event can bring considerable rewards to the BTL investor it's not a fore gone conclusion.

Check The Facts

Go to the planning office of the local council for the area in question and ask to see the local plan for that area. This will comprise of a number of plans including policies and proposals for; economy, employment, shopping, population and housing, environment, transport, community, recreation and leisure, public utilities, minerals, mixed use and regeneration.

These plans will show you exactly what is being proposed and is happening, rather than relying on information gleaned from the bloke with 10 pints and a kebab inside him you met outside the pub one evening. You'll remember when we were discussing the employment trigger event, how the media, businesses and other interested parties will talk something up or down as serves their interests best. This is why you must check the facts to find out what's really happening.

As well as just looking at the plans, talk with the planning officers. Find the most helpful one there and get as much information out of them as you can. It's from these plans and conversations that you build up a picture of what is really going on. If you've never heard the phrase "kite flying" used in this context now's the time to learn it. Some times a developer or company will make a noise in the media about an idea they have - but it is just an idea, not a solid proposal or anything remotely close - to see what the reaction will be. This is referred to as kite flying.

Talk

So you've confirmed that a potential trigger event is real and is scheduled to go ahead, now you want to talk with estate and letting agents and similar. People in the know. Find out what they believe will happen to the property market in the area in relation to the current position of that market. Find out the current supply and demand for property in that area. If there's already an over supply then a small increase in demand may not take up all of that slack so probably wouldn't make a good investment area.

What you really want to see is an area where demand already slightly outstrips supply so prices are already moving upwards. The trigger event might then amplify that movement. You need to analyse the trigger event to see what it's likely impact on that area will be. As well as talking with knowledgeable people in the property business (back to those agents again) you should also use your common sense.

As an example, if a new railway line is being constructed to a town outside a big city, common sense would suggest that this town will become more desirable for commuters which will cause house prices to rise. This is common sense. However, there is a little more to it than that. What is also common sense is that if you see the potential of this town developers are also going to see it and want to built new housing estates there. As a smart investor what you do is investigate land availability in and around that town. Back to the council offices.

You need to think from as many different points of view as you can. "What if I was a developer" and so on, follow these trains of thought through and investigate each one to see whether that area is still a good area to invest in.

Caution

Whilst trigger events are useful for us to investigate and can lead to big returns they certainly do not guarantee success.

Check that the project is definitely scheduled to go ahead (even when scheduled a project can still fall through, there is always some degree of risk in any investment). When at the council offices checking that the project is really scheduled to go ahead take the time to read the fine print and really understand what the proposed reality of the project is. The press hype could be somewhat different to what is actually going to happen.

As well as whether the project is scheduled you want to note when it's scheduled to happen and how long it'll take. Often planning permission is sought and gained for a project but then doesn't go ahead for years, or even at all. If you can find a time table take notes. Some of these projects will take decades to be completed and you might not want to wait that long to see some profit.

Another thing to bear in mind is with large construction projects there could be a lot of local noise and disruption which can have a depressing effect on house prices until the project is completed and it's benefits felt causing an uplift in house prices.

Keep tabs on the local media to gauge local opposition to the project (there will be some, every project has some opposition). Some opposition isn't usually too much of a problem but local opposition can prevent developments going ahead. At the tail end of the 80's the massive "Bridgehead 2000" development in Fife was eventually defeated, green belts created and existing ones enforced by coordinated local opposition.

A lot of the information gleaned from local councils will be proposals which introduces an element of risk as the trigger event may not actually happen in reality. There are always going to be risks so you must take these into consideration before investing. Another almost inevitable feature of these types of projects are delays. The larger the project the longer and more numerous the delays are likely to be.

Take To The Streets

Go to the area you're looking at and walk around it. You can get a much better feeling for an area when on foot than you can from driving through it. Pop into any estate agents you pass and have a chat with them. They will be able to tell you which are the more popular estates or roads within your target area which will be especially valuable information if you're not from that area and so don't have that local knowledge. Make sure you get more than one opinion on this, though. You don't want an agent telling you an area is popular because they've got a lot of houses to shift in that area!

Other local knowledge that you'll be interested in gaining relates to transport. Some housing estates may be better served by the local bus company than others, for example. Shops, health centres, recreational facilities, schools and many other things also go into making one area more popular than another. These are all things you can check. Ask in the local shop, the staff in these places are often a wealth of local knowledge and, of course, gossip. Always check your "facts".

Depending on your target market also look for potentially negative things like proximity to pubs and clubs. Great if you're going after a younger market, not so good if you're aiming to let a property to families.

You've already checked out the local plans, make sure you take your notes from the planning office with you on your walk about. Actually seeing the proposed site for some development or other can cast a very different light on it that you just can't see from the plans. Look at the location with your own eyes and have a think about how the plans stack up in that context.

Consequences

When looking to buy in an area based on a trigger event that promises to change the supply and demand ratio in your favour, causing a price increase then you need to assess for your self whether or not that trigger event will actually change the property market in your favour or not.

Take all your notes with you and go to the site. Look about and work out what will happen. Think through the construction and what impact that will have. For example a new railway line into town, see where it comes in, what will have to be demolished and so on. It could be that an area's car parking is going to be torn up or reduced in size which could cause the surrounding streets to fill up with parked cars making it difficult for the people who live in those streets and will probably push prices down. But then, there may be a multi-story car park planned at the new station just round the corner so once that's built the problem probably goes away. So there could be temporary negatives before longer term positives (and of course vice-versa).

Try and work out what sort of people the trigger event is likely to bring into the town, a rail link might bring an influx of young families - young professional couples now moving out of the city centre for a better quality of life for their new family, for example, but still need to commute to their jobs in the city, a new rail link could be right up their street.

It is a huge game of fortune telling and there will be factors you either couldn't know about or didn't think about. You can only work with the data you have and do your best. This is where the extra risk to your investment over and above the risk there always is with any investment is added.

20. Adding Value

As we've discussed, most BTL investors will want to bank the capital growth in their properties eventually. During the time the property is owned you may want to add some extra value to the property. This is over and above the normal maintenance you'd be doing any way, this is about adding value.

However, not all home improvements are equal when it comes to adding value and some will even potentially reduce the value of the property so it's important for us to discuss what's usually a good idea to do and what's normally a good idea to avoid.

Some of these things can be done to add value for tenants as well during the lifetime of your property ownership if you feel it's right for your situation. Some of them you'll probably not do until you're getting ready to sell the property.

Home Improvements, The Skinny

In the introduction to this chapter I said that not all home improvements are created equal when it comes to the value they add, or don't add. A classic example of this is a high spec. kitchen. You may be able to increase the rent a little (but possibly not even) and you may find a great kitchen helps you rent it out quicker (it is true, what they say, "kitchens and bathrooms sell houses") but even then it's pretty much guaranteed that you won't recoup all of your investment. That's obviously not a problem if you're lavishing the money on your own house and will get the non-financial benefits from it but in your BTL properties it's generally better to go with a cheaper, lower spec, option (but not shoddy) for the kitchen. You might get 75% of the cost back.

There are other home improvements, however, that can show a

decent return on investment. A classic example of this is a loft conversion. Because they add extra square metres to the property they have a very tangible value in that the space is either there or it isn't, unlike the level of spec. of a kitchen, a lower spec. is still a kitchen that you can cook in. You can usually charge more rent because the house will have more bedrooms (or at least more general space) and for the same reasons the sale value of the property will usually also increase. Obviously a lot depends on how you go about it but, if done sensibly, a loft conversion should not only pay for it's self it will often add value to the property over and above it's cost.

Those two examples above are fairly well at the two ends of the spectrum but there is also a greyer area in between. Improvements that don't necessarily add any significant value to the property or allow for increased rent but they help a property to sell faster or to let out faster (and possibly keep a tenant happier longer) such as landscaped gardens, for example.

Let's look at some examples of potential improvements in more detail...

Loft Conversions

Over a long period of time there have been numerous surveys conducted by all sorts of different organisations and they all pretty much agree that a loft conversion is, in most cases, a big value adder. When I say big I mean it can sometimes add as much as double it's cost. Eg. spend £20,000 on the work and the sale price of the property could increase by £40,000. Just to temper your enthusiasm a little here, don't bank on doubling your money with a loft conversion, that's a top end figure.

As with any project it needs to be well planned and executed to stand any chance of covering it's cost and adding additional value.

Firstly you need to plan things out. If you need to bring in professional help at this stage (an architect or surveyor) then do so but I'd recommend as the first step (as long as you feel you can make a decent enough fist of it to be worth while) getting some graph paper, a tape measure, ruler and pencil. Check with your local planning office for the current building regulations especially regarding ceiling heights for loft conversions. Carefully get up into the loft (if you are at all unsure as to how to move around in a loft space safely then don't do it, get some one in who can) and measure the space.

You want to measure the floor area, obviously, but also the height at the tallest part of the space (usually directly under the ridge line) and then at 1m intervals out towards the lowest edge. That way you know the slope of the roof and can find the point where the ceiling will be too low to be usable. Cupboards can be built into this otherwise "dead" area where the ceiling height would be too low for human use which can help with storage and not taking any of the human usable space away.

Draw it all out to scale as best you can on the graph paper and work out the human usable space available. The reason I recommend having a go at this your self to start with (again, only as long as you're confident about doing it and entirely at your own risk) is because if you find that the roof space simply isn't big enough to give you a decent amount of extra space that will justify the financial outlay then there's no point going any further, spending money on professionals to tell you it's not worth doing!

Assuming this stage goes well next you need to look at the floor below. Something people often forget to do. A loft conversion into living space requires a permanent staircase under current (at time of writing) building regulations, a loft ladder will not do. A stair case takes up space. You don't want to rob Peter to pay Paul, taking too much space from a bedroom, for example, to fit the stair case into to get the space back in the loft. That's pointless.

Sometimes it's possible to "stack" the new staircase above the existing one (obviously this doesn't apply in a bungalow setting) which can both save space and can make the staircase look like it's always been there. A good loft conversion should be in keeping with the look of the original building as much as possible, it should look like a natural part of the property. As well as the internal look, you don't want to ruin the curb-appeal of your lovely Edwardian property, for example, with a massive dormer sticking out of the roof. The extra space is a plus for buyers but if they hate the look they won't even cross the threshold let alone consider putting in an offer.

Back to the subject of ceiling heights, there needs to be enough extra space in the loft conversion with enough height to make that space comfortable for people to use regularly. Otherwise it just becomes a very expensive storage area.

If your own measurements and sketches stack up in your mind then it might be worth calling in the professionals to take things further. A proposed loft conversion may fail at another hurdle further down the line after money has been spent but at least if you can do a little planning initially this shouldn't happen as often as if you hadn't done any. You should be able to filter out the stark staring mad conversion locations.

Extensions

As with a loft conversion these can add significant value to a property. They're usually used to add an extra bedroom or two and/or to increase the size of a kitchen. They can also be used for extra bathrooms or even to increase general living space if the existing space is very small (extra general space tends to add less value than adding actual extra rooms though).

However, executed badly an extension can cost a great deal and add nothing to speak of to the value. A couple of examples of this might be adding a metre slice to the side of a house (very expensive for all that building work to gain very little extra space) or adding an extra bedroom to a 10 bedroom mansion (when you have that many already an extra one really isn't going to make any significant difference to the value).

Another parallel with loft conversions is that an extension should work as if it's part of the original property. For example an over-garage extension accessed off the existing landing rather than through another room and down a new corridor. That just doesn't work well.

Access to the new room or rooms is very important to consider at the planning stage. Avoid taking space away from an existing room to fit access into the new room/s as much as possible. The key is cost/benefit analysis. But not just financial cost, space cost too. Don't create another bedroom only to effectively lose an existing one by either chopping off so much for an access corridor it's unusable or turning it into a walk through to the new room. Neither of those generally work well. Walk-throughs are especially off-putting to most potential buyers.

Just watch some of these property programmes on TV and occasionally you will see some absolute howlers!

Measuring and drawing, just like we talked about for loft conversions, can help catch these sorts of things at the earliest stage (and further down the line a half decent architect should be able to avoid the more subtle issues for you as well). It can help you plan things out, play with different ideas and so on.

Another possible planning tool you might consider employing

is a large enough lawn or other area, a ball of string and some tent pegs or even twigs. Measure out full scale the extension with affected existing rooms and walk round them and try to visualise if they still work. If you've had to shave a bit off one, if you couldn't avoid it, make sure the extension's not going to have too big an impact on that room. Don't be afraid to call the idea off. "It'll be fine" isn't usually going to cut it!

Next add on the proposed extension floor plan. Walk about that as well, not forgetting to walk between the mapped out existing rooms/corridors and the extension. You're checking for that all important access. Check corridors are going to be wide enough, this is a common mistake made. They sound wide enough when the width is spoken and they might look acceptable on the plan but people often design corridors that turn out to be uncomfortably narrow in reality. Mapping out full scale often catches issues like this, it's well worth doing if you can.

Walk about the extension rooms and make sure they're going to work for their intended purposes. Even mark on the ground bed sizes, toilet and shower sizes and so on. Is there enough room to move about and to use these items? Having measurements for these items is a great help as often people underestimate the sizes of things. Kitchen worktops are quite a bit deeper than many people realise, for example.

A simple ball of string and a little time can save tens of thousands of Pounds!

Kitchens

We touched on this upgrade earlier as well. You may be able to recoup most of the cost of a new kitchen especially if you're replacing something very old-fashioned and/or battered. If you're replacing a perfectly serviceable kitchen then it's unlikely to recoup much of it's cost for you at all. Remember, you're not choosing a kitchen for your self, just because you don't like it doesn't mean your tenants won't so it's usually unwise to rip a reasonably modern kitchen out and replace it with another one.

Match the quality of the kitchen to the value of the property. What I mean here is that you don't want to put a hugely expensive, high spec, kitchen into a very average house, it just isn't going to increase the value of that house by much, at the end of the day it's still a very average house, just with a posh kitchen. Similarly like you wouldn't put a cheap kitchen into a very upmarket house - the potential buyer will spot it a mile off and will adjust their offer for the property accordingly. They're going to take into account how much a new kitchen of suitable specification and build quality will cost, and then probably add a bit more to the amount they take off their offer.

Even in an average house buyers normally want as roomy a kitchen as possible so you need to do everything you can to achieve as much in that direction as possible. It may be a cliché, but neutral colours. Keep it bland, light and soft and it will tend to look bigger.

Sometimes you will be able to simply replace the cupboard doors rather than the whole kitchen. Check to see the condition of the cupboard carcasses, if they're still good but the doors are tatty or very old fashioned just replace the doors. If you're really lucky you may be able to get away with painting cupboard doors if budget is really tight. It can freshen up the look of a kitchen.

A little more expensive than cupboard doors but still cheaper than replacing a whole kitchen, renewing the worktops is sometimes enough to revamp a tired looking kitchen. The combination of the two often works best though.

Replacing a vinyl floor doesn't have to cost a fortune and can really spruce up a kitchen. If the existing floor covering has tears, holes or even melted pan marks, replace it. If people see "germ traps" in a kitchen it usually turns them up and labels your whole house as "yuck!" in their minds.

Repainting walls in neutral colours, tiling (especially replacing cracked or broken tiles) and installing spotlights are all other things you might consider to refresh a kitchen and make it more appealing to potential buyers.

Renovating a kitchen is often more about ease of selling than adding absolute value. Although they can help considerably with attaining the best possible price for your property, they're just unlikely to elevate the price beyond what that type of house in that area is worth. However, don't forget that selling quickly has financial benefits as well.

Bathrooms

If you want a quick sale it's really time to get rid of that 70's avocado bathroom suite! Joking aside, if at all possible you want a white bathroom suite. It's a timeless classic. Clean and offends almost nobody. Another advantage of a white bathroom suite is that it reflects light and can help to make the room feel bigger.

If you're replacing the suite any way you may want to look at re-designing the bathroom. Buyers tend to find it unappealing to encounter the toilet as soon as they open the door. If possible re-position the toilet if it is immediately the first thing people see through the door.

Along with your white suite you'll want to use chrome or brass taps and other fittings, again these are pretty well timeless. They just stay in fashion.

Re-tiling can be a very cost effective way of rejuvenating a bathroom as well. You've guessed it, white tiles are usually the order of the day. You could add a few patterned or block colour "feature tiles" here and there to break up larger expanses of white tiles, to avoid it feeling too "clinical". Another way of doing this is with transfers which might be quicker, easier and possibly cheaper. Also it can be brought to a potential buyer's attention that they can be easily removed should they wish.

Moving onto that, frankly disgusting, 80's relic, bathroom carpet. If your bathroom is carpeted, rip it out and dispose of it. Get some vinyl flooring down or in a higher spec. environment tile it. Whatever is appropriate for the house. But definitely get rid of any carpet in a bathroom. Like we discussed with damaged flooring in a kitchen (and I should have mentioned back then, if (heaven forbid) the kitchen is carpeted get rid of it) a carpet in a bathroom has that "yuck!" factor as well. These days carpet in a kitchen or bathroom is seen as unhygienic. A vinyl floor covering doesn't have to cost the earth and will make a kitchen or bathroom massively more appealing than if there'd been a carpet in either.

Many people like to luxuriate in a hot bath now and then but these days a quick jump in the shower is what is required most of the time. Having a shower, even an over bath shower, in your bathroom is well worth while from a selling point of view. If space dictates that there's no bath tub that is a shame but not a deal breaker for most buyers but not having a shower can often cause people to think more than twice about putting an offer in.

Using a good looking combined towel rail/radiator not only saves space and provides warmth it can also add a little style to the room. If you can provide some storage in the bathroom that is a great selling feature. The usual places for this are under mirrors and basins. Storage close to the window is popular.

Flooring

This is a tricky one.

Some people suggest that laminate flooring can tip the balance between two identical houses. It's seen by some as cleaner and fresher than carpets. It is true that one person's taste in carpets isn't necessarily going to be another's and a potential buyer will factor into their offer the cost of immediately replacing carpets. Carpets can be stained or otherwise dirty. However, some people (my self included) absolutely despise laminate flooring. It's cold, slippery and noisy (a consideration in a flat, semi or terrace). Not to mention it's fake. I like a real wood floor but a fake plastic one? No-ta. So in that situation I'd be factoring in how much it'd cost to rip it up and carpet the place! May be I'm in a minority on that one although I have spoken to people who agree.

A chain of estate agents conducted a survey a few years back which suggested that laminate flooring throughout might increase the value by up to 5%, will it cost less than that to buy and fit? It's probably going to be a close call. Another thing to bear in mind, does it fit the house? Laminate flooring instead of real wood might feel a bit cheap and tacky in a beautiful, large, Victorian house with 15 foot ceilings! Also it'd be a good idea to make sure it isn't going out of fashion before spending the time and money on it.

Parking

The general rule of thumb when it comes to car parking is that the more built up the area is the more value off-road parking adds to the property. Obviously that's not true in every circumstance but generally it's the case. An off-road parking space is good, a garage is better. Some estimate that a parking space or single garage can add 6% or more to a property's value and a double garage as much as 15%. Those are average type numbers, so your property's individual circumstances will likely alter that.

The more urban the location the more benefit you're likely to see from parking, it's not usually such a big problem in a more rural location. Before building a garage or doing any earth moving for a parking space it's always a good idea to get a couple of estate agents to value your property and ask them how much of a difference to their valuation car parking would make. You may find spending a few thousand in the city is well worth it but not in a rural property. Find out before spending the money!

Another thing to check before you go ahead is planning. Check with your local council's planning office if you need any permissions or permits - you will likely be running cars over the pavement and that often requires permission. Also the council may insist that you have the curb lowered in front of it and there are more regulations surrounding that than you'd ever believe! It'll also cost you because the council will have to do it, it's highly unlikely you will be allowed to get your own contractor to do it. This cost must be factored in also.

Obviously prices vary but if you use an average price of £8,000 for the cost of adding a garage it should give you a starting point for your calculations (of course you'll get actual quotes from builders before committing to anything) and you'd hope to add around £15,000 to the value of the property. Again, check with estate agents to see how much it's likely to add before going ahead.

A word of caution, though. Adding a parking space or garage can reduce the value of the property as well, or at least make it harder to sell in some circumstances. It's a good idea to make the garage blend in with the house, use the same type of construction and same colour of bricks or whatever. But far more importantly, make sure it "works" with the property and it's plot. If the garage takes up a significant part of the garden then you're far less likely to sell to people with young families. They want a decent area of grass for their kids to rampage around on. You also want any garage to have enough room for a car to be parked in front of it and get the door open/closed. You don't want a garage to block access to the rear of the property either.

Before going ahead, look at it from the other side of the argument. Instead of what will it add to the property ask your self what it will take away from the property. Does it still sound like a good idea?

Swimming Pools

Just don't do it!

Whenever research is performed on this subject it comes back saying that a pool will not cover it's costs through added value but worse than that, they very often reduce the value of the property. If you spend 20 to 30 grand on installing a swimming pool really don't expect to see that back in the sale price of the property. A badly planned swimming pool will often reduce the actual value of the property. What I'm saying here is that in the normal run of things the best you can hope for from a swimming pool is that it won't devalue the property, because it's certainly not going to add value to it. You may find potential buyers are factoring in the cost of filling it in if they make an offer.

But why? There are a number of reasons cited for this, not least of all the maintenance costs of a pool. Running a pool is a costly business. There's cleaning, machinery maintenance, draining, filling and of course, heating. Then there are the less obvious down sides. Often a pool will have been built in what was the back garden. Families will definitely prefer a larger garden to a pool as will many other potential buyers. Then there's the safety issue. A pool is a constant worry for parents of small children.

Pick How You Add Value Carefully

This can be a little tricky to work out because different surveys on home improvements vary quite considerably in their findings. We're trying to categorise each type of improvement, whether it'll recoup it's costs and add value, just recoup it's costs or only recoup part of it's costs. Then there's whether it'll help the property to sell or not to add into the mix.

One such survey, by a mortgage lender, concluded that off-road parking and garages recoup their costs and add value and that:

Loft conversions, new bathrooms and new kitchens recoup about 75% of their costs.

Extensions recoup about 60% of their costs.

Conservatories recoup about 40% of their costs.

Double glazing and central heating recoup about 25% of their costs.

Garden landscaping recoups about 10% of it's cost.

However other surveys on the same subject conclude differently. Some even suggest that landscaping brings the best return and off-road parking the least.

So what to do about all this conflicting "evidence"? Basically, ignore it! Yep, the best course of action is to work out which value-adders are best for your specific property. Which one or ones are going to add the most value or have the biggest impact on saleability, depending on what you're going for.

For example. Say you have an inner city property most suited to young professionals where parking is murder then building a garage or parking space is far more likely to add value than landscaping the garden.

Conversely, if your property sits in extensive grounds then parking isn't going to be a problem so landscaping all that land may make the property far more appealing to potential buyers.

When you get those valuations we talked about earlier from at least two (but more is better) estate agents you'll also want to ask them how much market value would be for your property in perfect condition. This will help you ascertain whether it's worth spending more money on it or not. If your property is valued pretty close to the perfect condition value then you're going to add less value to the property by improving it. You could spend a fortune doing all sorts to your property without adding any significant value to it (although you might make it more saleable) because there is always a ceiling for that type of property in that area and no matter what you do to it you can't really break through that figure.

Take a 3 bed semi as an example. They're generally selling for £190k in the area. Yours has a loft conversion and you price it at £210k, £30k more. But at £210k you may have priced it into the next price bracket up - cheaper 4 bed properties. Most potential buyers looking to spend that much are going to go for the 4 bed rather than a 3 bed with loft conversion. So now you're trying to sell to the 3 bed semi market again, but for £30k more than other people are. That's going to be a tough sell.

I can't stress enough how important it is to gather as much information as possible before "pulling the trigger" on an improvement to add value. Get all the information you can from estate agents, get quotes from builders and talk over your plans with them as well, they may have good ideas too. Talk with your solicitor as well. The planning office at your local council should be visited too, don't forget to check building regulations whilst you're at it. You must make sure that your proposed value adder is actually going to achieve what you intended. Usually home improvements that add space bring the largest returns. But your property's individual circumstances may dictate a different tack, you have to assess what's right in that situation.

21. Summary

As a BTL investor you'll see BTL as a long term investment. In the short term your rental yield covers the mortgages and other outgoings and the big pay days come in the longer term when you sell a property on and reap the capital gains.

Profit Potential

You're using rents to cover your outgoings and cash in on capital growth at the end of that particular property's life in your portfolio. This means that you need a property that 1) will rent out easily, 2) will achieve sufficient rent to cover it's costs 3) will increase in value as much as possible over the next 10 or so years.

Since selling the property for it's capital gains is your exit strategy you must buy a property in an area where property prices are all but guaranteed to rise by a significant amount in the next 5 to 15 years. You must buy in a BTL hotspot that is set to continue as one so you can be sure of letting your property out for the duration of your ownership.

As you can see, you want your property in an area that is both a rental hotspot and a capital growth hotspot. If you buy in an area that is a rental hotspot but not a capital growth hotspot then you're not going to make a huge return on your investment when you come to sell. Buy in an area that is a capital growth hotspot but not a rental hot spot and in all likelihood you won't get to the stage of cashing in the capital gains, you'll have had to sell your empty property long before. This is why you need both.

Letting Hotspot

The thing that has the biggest impact on property prices (rents and sale price) is that supply and demand ratio. The principles are very simply, if there is high demand and insufficient supply then rents will be high. Conversely if supply outstrips demand then rents will fall. You need to buy property suitable to meet today's demand and tomorrow's. You're going to hold the property for 10 years or more in all probability so you need to buy such that you'll still be able to let it out then. That's the hard part of putting the simple supply and demand principles into practice.

You ideally want demand for that type of property in that area to increase during your ownership of it. University towns are particularly attractive to many BTL landlords due to this constant stream of tenant demand. Some of these BTL investors take that one step further and invest in towns where new universities are opening.

Having identified demand you must also assess the supply situation. You know what the demand is for so you can check what the supply for that type of property is like. Also check for the availability of building space in the area (go to the planning office) to make sure that a developer can't come in and fulfil that demand by building a new housing estate and flooding the market causing rents to drop and even not rent out in the first place.

Keep Your Tenants In Mind

Always, always remember that you're buying a property for your tenants, not for your self. Your preferences do not enter the equation. It's much easier to identify the largest and fastest growing type of tenant and then find a property to offer them than it is to buy a property you like and then try and find some one just like you to rent it from you - you've already got a house!

Probably the biggest group of people at this time is the late 20's/early 30's post-graduate group. They feel too old to be living in their parent's home but probably can't afford to buy anything just yet - especially when mortgages are so hard to obtain these days. Also they may not want to buy and prefer to rent for non-financial reasons. They probably don't want to be tied down by a house. They may want to go travelling or might foresee career movement within the next few years so renting is ideal for them.

In many areas this is your target market but of course you must check with local letting agents in the area you are targeting whether this is actually the case in that locality or not. It is vitally important to check, rather than making assumptions even if you know the area quite well. The letting agents will have a much better idea than you do of who's renting what, where. It is said that in Norwich there's a pretty clearly defined line with students renting on one side, near the University of East Anglia, and on the other side near the railway station it's all young couples and business executives.

Growth

As we've stated, supply and demand drive both the rental and capital growth aspects of the property market. A shortage of supply coupled with rising demand causes prices to rise. You'll not only want to see a shortage of supply but also a shortage of land that can be built on that would generate more supply.

You want to see the demand rising and as fast as possible. This rising demand puts further pressure on the limited supply. Rapidly rising demand can often be caused by some sort of trigger event. Rail development spreading out from the

"London 2012" site would have been a trigger event for those areas the new lines serviced. In the towns around dense urban areas transport links are usually the biggest form of trigger event. As travel to the large urban area becomes easier it sucks more towns into it's "commuter belt".

Triggers

We've already talked about transport links in the previous "Growth" section so we'll cover the others in this one.

A large new employer comes into the area is likely to trigger housing price rises. Some of the new jobs will probably be filled by locals but when thousands of jobs are created it always pulls people in from outside. People coming into a town they're not familiar with will almost always want to rent even if they plan to buy in the future so they can get a feel for the area before committing to buying somewhere. Also if they have to move in a hurry they won't want to rush their buying decision so, again, will want to rent first.

Schools opening can have an impact on property prices within it's catchment area as well. It's surprising how much parents will move around to get into the catchment area they want their children to be in. If a popular school has to relocate you'll also see quite a bit of movement from parents wanting their children to stay in that school. Should a good school spawn a sixth-form college it's likely to trigger some movement as well.

Far less tangible a trigger event is an area just becomes fashionable. It may sound daft but an area becoming fashionable for whatever reason or no reason at all, it just has, can see significant price rises. However, this can be fickle and areas can become unfashionable just as quickly.

Some signs of growth in an area include (but this is not an exhaustive list) the following types of business popping up:

Bistros, street cafés and the like.

Swanky restaurants.

Upmarket kitchen and bathroom shops.

Upmarket furniture shops.

You'll likely see the estate agents following as they sense they're onto a good thing in that area.

Conclusion

BTL is a wide and varied subject so one little manual like this can't possibly cover everything and discuss every eventuality but hopefully you have found it to be a solid introduction to the world of BTL.

Over a great many years, through boom times and busts, property has shown it is one of the bedrocks of investment success. Do it right and you can make a fortune to retire on. Do it badly and you can lose your shirt! There is always going to be risk no matter how careful you are but if you do as much due diligence as you possibly can you will minimise the risks as much as possible. So here's to your success over the next however many years, I sincerely hope you make a great return on your money and that this book has been the foundation of that success.

Bonus Chapter: Buying Property Abroad

I'm not recommending you start with buying property abroad, which is why I include this as a bonus chapter at the end.

Buying abroad can be both highly profitable and interesting so I wanted to give you a short introduction to it and to pass on some of the things I've learned about it. Also I hope to help prevent you from making some of the mistakes people often make when buying abroad.

People look to buying abroad for many reasons including those of life-style, retirement and investment. I heard a figure a while back of something around 1.5 million Britons now own property abroad and this number is set to balloon in the future.

Buying abroad can be very rewarding (whether it's financially or in life-style terms) but it isn't without it's issues. It is vital to be fully prepared before you buy and to check absolutely everything. To help you start that process I will give you ten tips...

Tip 1.

Research your intended country thoroughly. Find answers to the following questions:

What is the political situation in that country?

Is the local, legal, government stable?

Is the economy strong and stable?

Is the local currency strong and stable?

The Foreign and Commonwealth Office should be able to help you with these. Don't make any assumptions about a country that you may have come to from the news or the bloke down the pub. Check with the people who really know. Also the American CIA World Factbook can provide interesting information: https://www.cia.gov/library/publications/the-world-factbook

You need to find out and understand any local risks there may be in your country of choice. You also need to become familiar with the country's laws surrounding foreigners buying property. There may be restrictions (in some countries they are so severe it's just not worth bothering) or extra requirements that you must fulfil before being allowed to buy property there.

The residential property market in Northern Cyprus has experienced a boom time but it's definitely a case of "buyer beware". Many of the "bargain" properties foreign investors have been snapping up turn out to have disputed titles - it's not clear to any one who actually owns them. If you were to accidentally buy one of those it could have very big legal and financial implications for you.

Tip 2.

Once you have researched the country, it's governance and property laws/system and assuming that all went well you now need to research the area or areas you are considering buying into.

If you're buying for investment purposes then you need to thoroughly investigate what the local housing market is like. We'll come back to this in more detail in a moment.

If you're buying your holiday getaway then you absolutely

must take a holiday there for as long as you can. It's crazy the number of people who have just heard a place is nice and then buy themselves a holiday home there without having actually visited before. I have even heard of people selling up in the UK, buying somewhere abroad and moving there, on the strength of something they heard. They've never even visited. Utter madness!

On your holiday you will want to ascertain whether the climate suits you at the times of year you plan to be there. Whether the airport (or ferry port or however else you plan on getting there) is a sensible distance from your property. Whether the car rental facilities at the airport are sufficient. You should also check how long and how much effort it is door to door - from your house in the UK to the property abroad.

Something a startling number of Brits abroad don't even consider is the local language. "Every one just speaks English any way". Well I've got news for the people that say that, no they don't! If you're moving to a big city like Amsterdam, for example, then yes, you can very easily get away without learning Dutch. Move to rural France and it's a very different matter. Trust me, I've been to rural France and I don't speak a word of French. It was very difficult.

Back to investing abroad... You will want to rigorously investigate the local property market and all the local in's and out's.

What have house prices been doing over the last few years?

Is the market heading up or down?

Are there a lot of new developments planned?

Is demand going to continue to outstrip supply in that area for the foreseeable future?

Is the rental income going to cover the costs (you'll need to factor in your travel to and from as you're going to need to visit it occasionally)?

Will it rent out year round, if not how many months can you expect to have it let out? Will that number of month's rent cover the year's costs?

How easy will it be to rent out?

Whatever reason you're buying for - investment or lifestyle - you need to investigate the local amenities. Airports etc. for getting there and back home. Local transport for getting around. Shops. Doctors (see if you can find an English speaking one, unless your command of the local language is superb then it's very difficult being ill in a second language). Leisure facilities. Other amenities. Also consider schools if you're planning on letting it out to locals rather than as a holiday let for Brits.

Whilst the examples I've given so far have all been European many Brits have bought property in Florida. It's a huge place and as you'd expect there is also huge variation in the property market. Some areas are better than others for foreigners to invest in. Prices may have taken a beating but in time it's more than likely they'll rally, for example, Orlando has everything you'd want going for it - tremendous transport and other infrastructure, world class entertainment on tap and of course it's proximity to Disneyworld means it has exceptionally strong rental potential. Even if this changes by the time you come to buy there will be another scorching hot area.

Tip 3.

Get to grips with the local property buying process. Now you've checked out the country and area to buy in you need to fully understand the complete buying process as it applies to someone from the UK. Assume that the process is completely different to the one you're used to in the UK, so requires careful study. Any similarities are a bonus.

Estate agents and developers behave differently in different countries. Similar to the UK but probably more so, an estate agent (called "realtor") in the US will be acting entirely on behalf of the seller's best interests. In many southern European countries (especially the likes of Spain) you may find that a developer will just go ahead with their building project before they've got all the red tape squared away.

They may not have the relevant licenses, permits, permissions and so on. They work more on a mañana basis when it comes to the legal stuff. You must find out (don't just ask them, check whatever they say with the relevant authority) this information because without the relevant legal papers etc. you won't be able to get a mortgage on the property. Not to mention the fact that you could be forced to pull the building down if the legal stuff isn't done and the local authority don't want the building there. In some countries it's the local town's mayor that has almost dictatorial say in what is built and what isn't. If that's the case in the country you're planning on buying in it pays to keep in with the mayor!

See if you can find other Brits that have bought in that area and talk with them. Find out all you can from them. They will probably be able to warn you of the potential pitfalls, there's nothing like having gone through a process to truly understand it and know the problems. If you can't find other Brits then you'll have to try and chat up some of the locals.

Talk with local estate agents (or equivalent) and have them talk you through the process from beginning to end. They will also be able to paint you a picture of the state of the local housing market. If you can speak to more than one to try and weed out any hidden agendas.

As mentioned above, talk with the local authorities about the laws, permits and so on. Also about local tax laws. You really don't need a tax investigation going on over seas!

In hot spots where many Brits are buying you'll often find property businesses run by British people, set up specifically to cater for other Brits wanting to buy property. These have their advantages (especially when it comes to language and understanding the knowledge base you're coming from) but don't be fooled! Just because they speak the same language as you and you're comfortable with the accent doesn't mean that they're not shysters. Some of these companies are completely genuine but some are not. Some are just there to take unsuspecting fellow countrymen for a ride.

I'm not saying don't use one but if you do pick them very, very carefully. Do all the due diligence you can on them before engaging their services. If you can find people who have used them before you must speak with them and listen to their experiences. Also watch out for stooges. Some of these con-men are very sophisticated so you must take every precaution.

Tip 4.

Get to know the local market values. Do your due diligence here as well, research house prices in the area so you're not paying over the odds. Some people will try and take advantage of some one they think doesn't really know what's going on so you need to be prepared for that "special price" reserved for foreigners.

Drive about and just note down what you can get for how much money in the area. Get a feel for what is a fair price for what it is you're looking for. Turn your self from an ignorant buyer into an informed one.

When you're looking for a property, go round and talk with as many developers in the area so you know you're getting the best value for your money. If you have the money (and I'm not suggesting this for your first foreign purchase), you're confident and experienced then you can possibly start considering buying up whole developments at a time. You can work out some great discounts with the developer and build some relationships that can last years and make you both very wealthy indeed. But that's very much an "advanced" strategy when you have quite a few individual purchases in that country under your belt.

Tip 5.

Just as you would when buying an existing property in the UK you should always have a survey carried out on the building. If you're buying from a developer, as we talked about above, you must investigate them as much as you can. You don't want to have signed contracts only to find out that the foundations are insufficient and the roof leaks.

For this research a couple of good starting points would be the local records office and of course the local chamber of commerce, or equivalent.

Another thing you'll want to do is find out the location of some of his other developments and inspect them to get a feel for build quality.

You've probably heard at least one of the many horror stories about foreign developers going bust, taking investor's money with them. You should always insist on developer's insurance being in place (and periodically check it) before even considering doing business with them.

Tip 6.

Because buying property involves a raft of legal stuff you should engage the services of a good quality, local, independent solicitor/lawyer/equivalent. You'll want to find one that speaks English fluently, legal matters are not something you want to practice your language skills on if you're only just learning the local language. Even if you're fairly fluent it would be advisable to use an English speaking legal representative. It goes without saying that they must also be fluent in the local language (in the cases where you might find an immigrant lawyer). Have them do all the legal research that is required.

Chose this person well as they will be the most critical person in the whole endeavour. They will be able to provide you with advice at every stage. It is their job to make sure all the legal paperwork such as permits, permissions, titles and so forth are in place, genuine and binding. Also that there isn't any hidden debt tied up in the property that you would end up being liable for. They can advise you under who's name the property should be registered which can be important in certain circumstances.

Something to note, in some countries including France and Spain a "notary" is not a solicitor like you'd find in the UK. They're a public official who won't always volunteer you advice.

Tip 7.

Have your finances in order before you start. Make sure you know how you're going to pay for the property. Make sure you know how much you can afford. Those both may sound stupidly obvious but you'd be amazed how many people find the perfect property and then try and work out how they're going to pay for it.

Some people will be selling their UK home and moving permanently. That's pretty straight forwards. Most people will either be buying a holiday home or investment property so will likely be re-mortgaging their UK home. You need to know how much you can re-mortgage for and how you're going to fund the payments. May be rental income from your UK portfolio will fund it. Don't forget the ongoing maintenance costs and any local taxes, ground rents and so on that you'll have to pay. For a holiday let you will also need to employ a local house keeper to clean the property and launder the bedding/towels etc. between lets.

You will find that many other countries are like the UK in that a lump sum deposit is required. You'll need to have that in place ready. Make sure you're familiar with all the local taxes and fees you may be required to pay for owning property in that area and factor in maintenance costs as well. If you're planning on letting it out you'll almost certainly want to employ a local letting agent who will also require payment.

Think ahead as well. Find out how much estate agents will charge to sell your property. In some countries they charge a whole heap more than they do in the UK. In Spain, for example, you may find your self being charged 10 or even 15% instead of the 2% or so you'd expect in the UK. There are other methods of selling houses in these countries but if you are going to go the estate agent route then you'll have to factor in their large fees.

Exchange rate fluctuations add another level of complication to the process. When talking about the sorts of sums of money involved in property even a small change in the exchange rate can make a big difference. Your financial plan will need to allow for a certain amount of fluctuation. Setting up and using a local bank account may help when it comes to paying monthly bills for the property. You can set up standing orders and so on and of course with internet banking it's never been easier to remotely administer a bank account. Whilst you would always pay your bills on time it's worth knowing the penalties for not doing so. In some countries non-payment of taxes can lead to property seizure after court proceedings.

Tip 8.

Learn about all the different mortgage options available to you and work out which one will suit your needs best. You may or may not be able to get a local mortgage from a local bank but many Brits buying abroad get a UK mortgage designed for buying international property. Use a decent mortgage advisor who's familiar with UK mortgages for buying property abroad. They can advise you of the best way to go for the property and area it's in. Whether to get a Sterling mortgage or a local currency mortgage, for example.

When dealing with the money make doubly sure you're dealing with reputable companies. It wouldn't be the first time people have paid a deposit and then not been able to raise the remainder of the money. They didn't have a "get out clause" in the contract and ended up losing their entire deposit.

Tip 9.

Take professional advice on the subject of inheritance law and tax both in the UK and in the country you're buying in. They should be able to help you plan in the most tax efficient manner. You will probably find you have to draw up a local will to ensure your assets in that country are disposed of as you want rather than in accordance with local legal custom.

The French inheritance system is infamous. From time to time noises do come out of France about overhauling their arcane inheritance law but don't hold your breath on that one! If you have assets in France and you die you'd probably expect your spouse to inherit. Not so. The assets will usually be split up between your parents and siblings. Even if you have drawn up a French will the proportion of the assets that can be given to your surviving spouse is severely limited. One possible way round French inheritance law is to buy the property jointly with your spouse and also have a French will drawn up with professional advice throughout.

Foreign (especially French) inheritance law can be a complete minefield which is why it's very important to investigate it thoroughly before investing and to seek professional advice.

Tip 10.

Get your insurance sorted out. Make sure you fully cover the property for the purpose you intend it for. A general policy is unlikely to cover it for rental use. Holiday use may not even be covered by a general policy because it's empty quite a bit of the time. You may need special holiday property insurance. It's never a good idea to "embroider the truth" or keep anything back from insurance companies. It may save you a few quid on your monthly premiums but should you ever need to make a claim they can simply wash their hands of it because you didn't give them the correct and full information.

Some Final Thoughts

Whether buying to let in the UK or abroad, your preferences are completely irrelevant. Buy the property without emotion, based entirely on facts and figures. A good analogy for an investment property is a box that makes money. If you were buying some sort of magical box that spat out money from the magic money box shop you would want to pick the one that gave you the best return on your investment. You wouldn't care what shape or colour it was. Your property box is just the same.

You might think that all the research, planning, maintenance and so on that goes into successful property investment is a lot of time, effort and hassle but think again. In a "normal" job you'd probably be working 8 hours a day, 5 day's a week and getting two or three weeks a year off. Does it really still sound like a lot of work now we're putting it in perspective? It is easier if you work with a partner (business or romantic!) but it is still possible to go it alone.

Think about this... You could put in some hard graft building up your property portfolio over, say 5 years, continue managing it for another 5 to 10 years and have a great retirement nest egg at the end of it. Or you could spend 30 years of your life working for The Man and have a miserable pension doled out to you every month that barely allows you to keep the heating on in winter. Surely a little bit of effort now in getting your BTL purchases right is well worthwhile?

A lot of wannabe investors see a few property programmes on TV and truly believe they can wander into a "deal of the century" situation and be set for life. As a seriously committed investor (which you seem to be, having got this far) you'll know that's highly unlikely and it takes time, effort and determination to be successful. You're going about things the right way, educating your self first.

Now you've read about the basics in this book and have a few pointers you can further your property education and with any luck make a roaring success of your property investment. However, you can do all the reading in the world but at the end of the day there's nothing you can read in a book quite like actually doing something. You will learn far more from your first few investments than you could ever hope to from books and experts. Reading this book and others like it is very, very important to give you a basis and help you avoid making the more common mistakes but actually doing it is always going to give you a better education.

Here's to your success and I wish you the very best for your investment future.

James Collier.

Useful Names & Addresses

I have included a directory of useful names, addresses and web addresses. Companies and organisations move from time to time so it's worth while checking before posting anything.

The Conveyancing Association

3 Priory Court

Pilgrim Street

London

EC4V 6DR

020 7618 9141

http://www.theconveyancingassociation.co.uk

National Association of Estate Agents

Arbon House

6 Tournament Court

Edgehill Drive

Warwick

Warkickshire

CV34 6LG

0845 250 6001

http://www.naea.co.uk

Royal Institution of Chartered Surveyors

RICS HQ

Parliament Square

London

SW1P 3AD

024 7686 8555

No's. for their UK regional offices can be found on their website.

http://www.rics.org/uk

Incorporated Society of Valuers & Auctioneers

Now merged with:

Royal Institute of Chartered Surveyors (above).

The Law Society

113 Chancery Lane

London

WC2A 1PL

020 7242 1222

http://www.lawsociety.org.uk/

Scotland: http://www.lawscot.org.uk

Northern Ireland: http://www.lawsoc-ni.org

Association of Residential Letting Agents

Arbon House

6 Tournament Court

Edgehill Drive

Warwick

Warkickshire

CV34 6LG

0845 250 6001

http://www.arla.co.uk

Federation of Master Builders

Gordon Fisher House

14-15 Great James St

WC1N 3DP

020 7242 7583

http://www.fmb.org.uk

Royal Town Planning Institute

41 Botolph Lane

London

EC3R 8DL

020 7929 9494

http://www.rtpi.org.uk

Royal Institute of British Architects

66 Portland Place

London

W1B 1AD

020 7580 5533

http://www.architecture.com

Institute of Structural Engineers

11 Upper Belgrave St

London

SW1X 8BH

020 7235 4535

http://www.istructe.org

Printed in Great Britain
by Amazon.co.uk, Ltd.,
Marston Gate.